SELLING YOUR
BUSINESS
TO AN
ESOP

Tenth Edition

Selling Your Business to an ESOP

Tenth Edition

Bill Brett
Christopher J. Clarkson
Ronald J. Gilbert
Stacie Jacobsen
Nathan Nicholson
Loren Rodgers
Corey Rosen
Paige A. Ryan
Kenneth E. Serwinski
Brian B. Snarr

The National Center for Employee Ownership
Oakland, California

This publication is designed to provide accurate and authoritative information in regard to the subject matter covered. It is sold with the understanding that the publisher is not engaged in rendering legal, accounting, or other professional service. If legal advice or other expert assistance is required, the services of a competent professional person should be sought.

Legal, accounting, and other rules affecting business often change. Before making decisions based on the information you find here or in any publication from any publisher, you should ascertain what changes might have occurred and what changes might be forthcoming. The NCEO's website (including the members-only area) and newsletter for members provide regular updates on these changes. If you have any questions or concerns about a particular issue, check with your professional advisor or, if you are an NCEO member, call or email us.

Selling Your Business to an ESOP, Tenth Edition
Book design by Scott Rodrick

Copyright © 2017 by The National Center for Employee Ownership. All rights reserved. No part of this book may be reproduced or transmitted in any form or by any means, electronic or mechanical, including photocopying, recording, or by any information storage and retrieval system, without prior written permission from the publisher.

Originally published as *Selling to an ESOP* in 1996. Second edition, 1997. Third edition, 1988. Fourth edition, 1999. Fifth edition, 1999. Sixth edition, 2000; revised printing, 2001. Seventh edition, 2002. Eighth edition, 2005. Ninth edition, titled *Selling Your Business to an ESOP*, published in April 2012. Tenth edition, February 2017.

The National Center for Employee Ownership
1629 Telegraph Ave., Suite 200
Oakland, CA 94612
(510) 208-1300
(510) 272-9510 (fax)
www.nceo.org

ISBN: 978-1-938220-44-9

Contents

Preface

Myths and misconceptions prevent many owners of closely held businesses from considering selling their companies through an employee stock ownership plan (ESOP). For many such owners, ESOPs have advantages in terms of tax, financial, and intangible issues that no other transaction method can offer.

The alternatives to an ESOP sale, while appropriate for some business owners, may not be feasible or may have disadvantages that make them unpalatable to others. For example, a sale to a third party often results in protracted negotiations with someone who does not view the corporation in the same way the owner does and who may have no concern for the welfare of the employees, the community, or the legacy of the company. Third-party sales rarely allow the owner to sell a partial interest and may impose substantial constraints on the seller. An initial public offering (IPO) is available to only a select group of companies in the U.S. and imposes time constraints on when the owner can "sell out" after the IPO. Management buyouts are intriguing, but the actual nuts and bolts of making them happen, especially financing, will derail many such transactions.

An ESOP can provide a market for a closely held business, which can be sold to the ESOP either as a going concern or in stages. The ESOP also provides significant tax incentives for the selling shareholder, the corporation that establishes the ESOP, and the employees of the corporation. Additionally, companies that combine broad-based employee ownership (as through an ESOP) with employee participation programs tend to show substantial performance gains.

This book is designed to educate owners, managers, and advisors of closely held businesses on selling to an ESOP. The first chapter describes how ESOPs work and what the basic rules are, while the second reviews the alternatives to an ESOP and situations where an ESOP might or might not be a good fit. The next three chapters cover the important topics of valuation, leveraged ESOP financing, and ESOP feasibility. The seller's post-transaction concerns are addressed in the following chapters on investing the sale proceeds, one seller's investment decisions, and the prohibited allocation rule under Section 1042. The final chapter discusses the results of the NCEO's 2015 ESOP Transaction Survey.

In this 10th edition, chapters 1 to 5 and chapter 8 have been revised and updated where appropriate, two new chapters (6 and 7) replace the former discussion of investing the sale proceeds, and chapter 9 on the transaction survey has been added.

We at the NCEO hope that you enjoy this book and that it inspires you to evaluate carefully the benefits of employee ownership through the use of an ESOP. Visit our website at www.nceo.org for more information and resources on ESOPs.

Chapter 1

An Introduction to ESOPs

Corey Rosen

Bob Moore, the owner of Bob's Red Mill, had built his provider of whole-grain flour and other products into an iconic national brand. He could have sold to any number of buyers, but that just didn't seem right. So on his 81st birthday, he made an announcement to his 200 employees. The company would now be theirs, thanks to an employee stock ownership plan (ESOP). "It's been my dream all along," he said, "to turn this company over to the employees, and to make that dream a reality is very, very special to me. This is the ultimate way to keep this business moving forward. I get to spend every day with our many loyal and long-time employees who will now share in ownership, and it just thrills me to know they will be joined by many new faces over the years."

The story was picked up by CNN, PBS, and the wire services and soon appeared all over the country. To the media, what Bob Moore did seemed extraordinary, but, in fact, it was just one more example of a now very commonly used approach for owners of closely held companies to deal with business transition.

One of the most difficult problems for owners of closely held businesses is finding a way to turn their equity in a business into cash for retirement or other purposes. The decision to sell is more than an economic one, however. After putting years of his or her life into a business, an owner develops a strong feeling of identity with the company. At the same time, the owner often has a sense of loyalty to the employees and would like to see them have a continuing role in the company. Still other owners only want to sell some ownership, or to buy another owner out. Selling a partial interest in a company is very hard to do. Redemptions and sales to employees are possible, but must be done in expensive after-tax dollars.

For some business owners, the answer to these problems will be to turn over the company to an heir, sell to managers, or sell to a competitor. But many owners do not have heirs interested in the business or managers who have both the interest and the money to buy the company. The right outside buyer can be hard to find. Even if they can be found, they may want to buy the company for its customer lists, technology, or facilities, or may just want to put a competitor out of business. As the next chapter shows, the offers these outside buyers make are often not nearly as good as they may seem.

ESOPs can be a very attractive and tax-favored alternative. ESOPs can do things that cannot be done any other way. That is what Congress intended. For example:

- In an ESOP, employees do not have to use their after-tax dollars to buy company stock (and almost never do). Instead, the company can make tax-deductible contributions to an employee stock ownership trust to enable the trust to buy the owner's shares.

- Because the contributions a company makes to an ESOP are deductible, that means ESOPs are unique in allowing companies to use pretax dollars to buy one or more owner's shares.

- For the owner of a C corporation, taxes on the proceeds from the sale to the ESOP can be indefinitely deferred (if certain conditions are met) by reinvesting in the securities of other domestic companies. If these securities are not sold before the owner's death, no capital gains tax is ever due. If the company is an S corporation, LLC, or partnership, it can convert to a C corporation before the sale to take advantage of this tax deferral.

- If the company is an S corporation and remains one, the owner does pay capital gains tax on the sale but reaps all the other benefits of selling to an ESOP. In addition, once the ESOP is an owner, whatever profits are attributable to the ESOP are not taxable.

- The sale can be all at once or gradual, for as little or as much of the stock as desired. For the employees, no contributions are required to purchase the owner's shares. The owner can stay with the business in whatever capacity is desired.

- The plan is governed by a trustee who votes the shares, but the board appoints the trustee, so changes in corporate control are usually nominal unless the plan is set up by the company to give employees more input at this level.

- The ESOP can be financed in several ways: by periodic, discretionary cash contributions; by money borrowed from an outside lender; or by a note the seller takes from the ESOP. However the ESOP is financed, the company contributions to the plan are still tax-deductible.

In return for these substantial benefits, ESOPs need to meet certain requirements that ensure the benefits of the plan are provided in an equitable manner to employees. ESOPs are not a way to provide ownership to specific people, nor can they allocate ownership based on merit or some other discretionary formula.

ESOPs are not for every company. If you cannot live with their legal requirements, you need to look at alternative approaches to transition. If your company is not now or will not soon be profitable enough to fund its ongoing obligations and the nonproductive expense of buying out an owner, an ESOP just won't work. If you do not have successor management, the company will have difficulty paying off an acquisition debt it takes on and probably will not get a loan anyway. ESOPs also are more complicated than other benefit plans, and come with significant legal, administrative, and valuation costs, albeit these costs are a great deal less than what a business broker would charge. Contrary to what you might have heard, however, ESOPs do not work best only if you are in a certain industry, are fairly large (ESOPs can work in companies with as few as 10 or 20 employees), or have certain kinds of employees. Nor do they require, as noted above, that employees will now run the company.

This chapter provides a general overview of how ESOPs work for business transition. For those who want to look at some of the specific rules and regulations, the footnotes provide references.

What Is an ESOP?

An ESOP is a kind of defined contribution employee benefit plan, similar in some ways to other defined contribution plans such as 401(k) plans.

Each participant in a defined contribution plan has an account in the plan trust. The assets build up in each account based on contributions from the employer and/or employee. The employee generally gets these assets some time after leaving the company. Defined benefit plans, in contrast, are what we often think of as pension plans—plans where the benefit employees get is defined in advance, and the employer then has to provide enough funding to pay for it. Employees do not have individual accounts but instead are paid a specific monthly amount in retirement, usually based on factors such as salary history and years of service.

In an ESOP, as in other defined contribution plans, a company sets up a trust fund, into which it contributes new shares of its own stock or cash to buy existing shares. Alternatively, the ESOP can borrow money to buy new or existing shares, with the company making cash contributions to the plan to enable it to repay the loan (this is called a "leveraged" ESOP). Regardless of how the plan acquires stock, company contributions to the trust are tax-deductible, within certain limits. If shares or cash are contributed directly, they are immediately allocated to employee accounts. If the trust borrows money to buy shares, the shares first go into a "suspense account." Then, as the shares are paid for, they are released to employee accounts.

Generally, employees become eligible for the plan by working at least 1,000 hours or more in a plan year (as with all ESOP rules, the plan can have more liberal requirements). They get allocations based on relative pay or a more level formula, vest in their allocations over time, and get distributions of their accounts at defined points after they leave or, in some cases, are eligible to diversify their accounts before leaving. These rules are described in more detail later in this chapter.

An ESOP is governed by a trustee appointed by the board of directors, and employees are required to have only minimal voting rights. Managers are still managers, and, with a very limited number of exceptions, ESOPs only result in a change in corporate governance when the company voluntarily chooses to do so. In closely held companies, all ESOP transactions must be based on the stock's fair market value as determined by an outside, independent appraisal. These issues are also explored in more detail below.

Having an ESOP does not preclude a company from compensating key employees in any manner that would otherwise be reasonable and justifiable. Managers can get grants of stock options or synthetic equity (phantom stock and stock appreciation rights, for example), incentive pay, deferred compensation, and normal perquisites. An ESOP trustee should object only if this compensation amounts to a waste of corporate assets. Of course, any equity claims on the company, such as stock options or phantom stock that represent potential dilution, will affect valuation. In practice, ESOP companies tend to be conservative in how they pay management. The NCEO book *Executive Compensation in ESOP Companies* explores this issue in detail and includes the results of a survey of company practices.

Tax Benefits

Because the tax benefits of an ESOP are often a major (but not by far the only) driver of these plans, it is important to discuss in more detail just what they are and how they work.

Company Contributions to the Plan Are Tax-Deductible, Within Limits

Generally, money the company contributes to the ESOP to be used to purchase shares from an owner is tax-deductible, whether the contribution is made periodically in cash or the trust borrows money and the company puts cash into the plan to enable the trust to repay the loan.[1] There are two sets of limits, however. First, there are limits on the total amount that can be contributed. All ESOP companies can make tax-deductible contributions of up to 25% of the aggregate "eligible pay"[2] of employees in the plan (or plans), regardless of whether the ESOP is leveraged or not, or in a C or S corporation. This 25% limit, however, includes all of a company's contributions to its defined contribution plans (ESOPs, stock bonus plans, profit sharing plans, and 401(k) plans), with the exception of leveraged ESOPs, which can actually ignore other plans, as explained below. Contributions to defined benefit plans do

---

1. Contributions to the plan for other purposes are deductible as well, such as contributions of shares or straight cash contributions to provide a cash account for employees in the plan.
2. Revenue Ruling 80-145 defines eligible pay.

not count toward this limit. In C corporations, when there is an ESOP loan, only contributions used to repay principal count toward the 25% of pay limit; in S corporations, contributions to pay both principal and interest count.[3] Distributions of earnings used to repay an ESOP loan in S corporations do not count toward the 25% limit, nor do dividends used for this purpose in C corporations.

Second, there are limits on how much can be added to any one employee's account each year, called the "maximum annual addition." This cannot exceed the lesser of 100% of any plan participant's pay or $54,000 in 2017 (this figure is indexed annually for inflation in $1,000 increments). In C corporation ESOPs, dividends used to repay a loan do not count toward the annual addition limit, nor do contributions used to pay interest. Employee deferrals (except for "catch-up" contributions by those age 50 or older) also count toward the annual addition limit. Annual additions thus include practically all employer and employee contributions to defined contribution plans. In S corporations, interest payments and forfeitures of unvested account balances count toward the annual addition limits, but distributions do not.[4]

All of these requirements refer to "eligible pay." Eligible pay is the total payroll used in calculating the above limits, excluding pay over $270,000 per employee (as of 2017; this figure is indexed annually for inflation). Some people who work for you will not be in the plan, so their pay does not count; others may be in the plan, but are not eligible to receive an allocation of stock.[5]

These limits rarely raise issues, however. In C corporation ESOPs, if there is a leveraged ESOP, it is possible to have separate 25% limits for the leveraged ESOP and for other defined contribution plans, including a non-leveraged ESOP. That means a company could contribute up to

---

3. Section 404 of the Internal Revenue Code (the "Code"), especially Section 404(a) for contributions to defined contribution plans generally and Section 404(a)(9) for contributions to repay an ESOP loan.

4. Code § 415(c) and (j) discuss the issues raised in this paragraph.

5. This includes people who have not yet met your eligibility rules, people who are excluded from the plan (see the section on eligibility later in this chapter), and, for owners taking advantage of the tax-deferral features of selling to an ESOP in a C corporation, those who by law cannot get any of the stock in the ESOP that is subject to the tax deferral (the owners who elect the tax deferral, certain family members, and more-than-25% shareholders).

50% of eligible pay to its defined contribution plans.[6] As noted above, dividends (in C corporations) and distributions used to repay ESOP loans (in S corporations) also do not count toward the limits. Finally, ESOP companies usually also set up a leveraged ESOP so there is a loan from a lender to the company that is reloaned to the ESOP. This so-called "inside" loan can have longer terms than the "outside" (lender to company) loan, thus spreading the needed contributions to repay a loan over a longer period of time.

Dividend Deductibility

In C corporations, "reasonable" dividends[7] on ESOP-held stock that are used to repay an ESOP loan, that are passed through to participants, or are reinvested by participants in company stock in the ESOP are tax-deductible.

When C corporation dividends or S corporation distributions are used to repay an ESOP loan, the money put into the plan releases shares that have not yet been paid for, which are then allocated to employee accounts. Dividends or distributions that are paid on shares already allocated to employee accounts (those that have been paid for) release shares pro-rata to the percentage of shares held in each account; dividends or distributions paid on shares not already paid for can release shares to participant accounts based on relative account balances or on the company's usual allocation formula (most commonly, relative pay). Dividends or distributions on allocated shares used to repay an ESOP loan must be used to release shares with a value at least equal to the dividend or distribution.[8] Most companies use the latter approach to avoid a variety of potential problems beyond the scope of this discussion.

Tax Deferral for the Sellers (the Section 1042 "Rollover")

Owners of stock in closely corporations who have held that stock for at least three years before the sale to an ESOP can defer taxation on

---

6. PLR 200436015.

7. Code § 404(k).

8. Code § 404(k)(2)(B) (for C corporations); Code § 4975(f)(7) (for S corporations).

their gain by reinvesting in what are called "qualifying securities." No capital gains tax is then due until these new investments are sold. If some are sold, then the tax is pro-rata to that portion of the portfolio. In any case, the basis for calculating future capital gains tax is the basis in the ownership interest that was sold to the ESOP. If the taxes are held until death, the basis is stepped up, but estate taxes would apply.[9] You may often hear of this benefit referred as a "1042 transaction" because Code Section 1042 governs it.

There are several requirements to get this special treatment:

1. The company must be a C corporation at the time of sale.

2. Corporations cannot sell to an ESOP and elect Section 1042 treatment, but partnerships, limited liability corporations (LLCs), estates, taxable trusts, and individual owners can.

3. Ownership interests must have been held for at least three years before the sale to the ESOP. The shares sold to the ESOP do not qualify if they were acquired as part of an employee benefit plan or though certain types of stock options. If a company is an S corporation, LLC, partnership, or sole proprietorship, then converts to C status before the sale to an ESOP, the owner's prior holding period counts toward the three-year limit.

4. The ESOP must end up owning at least 30% of the total value of shares or 30% of each class of shares in the company after the sale. Any subsequent sales qualify as well. You may hear some ill-informed advisors say that *all* ESOPs must own at least 30% of the stock. That is not the case. The 30% rule is relevant only if the seller wants to defer taxation.

5. Proceeds must be reinvested in qualifying securities, defined as stocks and bonds of U.S. corporations that do not earn more than 25% of their income from passive investment. You cannot invest in mutual funds, government bonds, and other securities that do not meet these tests and still get a deferral.

---

9. The tax law in 2010 was an anomaly in that the step-up in basis was limited and there were no estate taxes.

6. Any direct family members (brothers, sisters, children, parents, spouses) of the selling shareholder(s) and any more-than-25% owners (as of the sale date) cannot receive an allocation in the ESOP of any of the shares that are subject to the deferral.

7. If within three years of the sale, the total number of shares held by the ESOP is less than the total held immediately after the Section 1042 acquisition of stock by the ESOP trust, or the value of the trust's ownership drops to below 30% of the value of all the shares in the company, then the company pays a 10% excise tax. There are exceptions to this rule, however, for changes in ownership due to certain distributions of shares to participants or a tax-free exchange of securities in another company (typically, as part of a sale of the company).[10]

Deferral of Tax for Plan Participants

As with participants in other qualified retirement plans (401(k) plans, profit sharing plans, etc.), employees are not taxed on anything the company puts into the plan, nor any appreciation in its holdings, until they receive a distribution, and, even then, they can roll that into an IRA if they are still at an age where they are eligible to do that.

Even If the Seller Does Not Elect the Section 1042 Tax Deferral, the Gain Is Treated as a Capital Gain, Not a Dividend

If a seller redeems stock to a company, it is often treated as a qualified dividend. As of this writing (2016), federal qualified dividend and long-term capital gains rates are the same, but that could change in future years. In the past, dividends have been taxed at the same rate as ordinary income.

Non-Tax Benefits of Selling to an ESOP

For Bob Moore (the company owner discussed at the beginning of this chapter), the tax benefits of an ESOP were good to have, but the

---

10. Code § 4978(d).

real drivers were his attachment to the company, its purpose, and its employees. There is no guarantee that another buyer would honor any of that, and they often don't.

In fact, using ESOPs as a business transition tool offers a variety of benefits beyond taxes:

- *You can sell all or some of your ownership interest and leave the company on your own schedule:* Other buyers usually want to buy the whole company. They may not want you to be involved any further, or they may require that you stay involved to some extent even if you do not want to do that.

- *If there are multiple owners, the ESOP can buy shares only from those who want to sell:* When there is more than one owner, one may be ready to sell and, perhaps, retire, while others may not be ready. Outside buyers do not want partners in most cases, so everyone has to sell. If an inside buyer purchases the stock, it is all with after-tax dollars.

- *The company will retain its identity:* Many owners have worked hard and long to build a good name for their company. Seeing it vanish into another company, and, in some cases, move outside the community, can be painful.

- *Even after you sell, you can stay involved:* Many former owners retain a board seat or some other involvement with the company for some period of time.

- *Employees who helped build the company now own it:* Many owners have a strong sense of loyalty to their employees and hate the idea of their becoming employees of another company, where they might not be treated well and often would be asked to leave. That is especially true at the senior level.

Financing the ESOP

ESOPs can be financed by an outside loan, a seller note, company cash contributions, dividends (C corporations) or distributions (in S corporations), or, rarely, employee contributions. These approaches can also be combined. The sale can also involve non-ESOP buyers, such as investors and/or managers who buy stock in the conventional way. ESOPs can buy all or a part of the stock in a company. Often, ESOPs are done in stages, buying some stock now and some after the first acquisition is paid for.

Mechanics of Leveraged ESOP Financing

In a leveraged ESOP, the ESOP borrows money to buy shares. In the typical transaction structure, the loan is made to the company. The company then reloans the funds to the ESOP. The terms of the two loans do not have to be identical. The "inside" loan (from the company to the ESOP) may be repaid over a longer period of time if that helps the company stay within the contribution limits or helps spread the annual contributions so most of the benefits of the ESOP are not captured in the first several years, but remain available to future employees as well.

Stock acquired by the plan goes into a suspense account. As shares are paid for, they are released to employee accounts. The amount paid for by company contributions can be released based on the percentage of principal repaid or the total principal plus interest repaid (the latter method is required for loans of 10 years or longer). Dividends or distributions can also be paid and would release additional shares (the mechanics of this are discussed in the section below on rules relating to participants).

Bank Financing

Outside lenders, such as banks, look for much the same collateral they would seek in a conventional loan, but if a seller is selling to an ESOP, there is insufficient collateral, and the seller is electing Section 1042 treatment, they may also ask for the seller's replacement security investments (the stocks and bonds the seller buys with the proceeds of the sale) to be pledged against the loan.

Seller Financing

Sellers often just take a note to finance an ESOP. As discussed later in this chapter, this raises special issues for sellers wanting to take advantage of the Section 1042 tax deferral, but those issues can be managed. Seller notes could be directly to the ESOP or to the company and then reloaned to the ESOP (the latter provides more flexibility). The seller can charge an arms-length equivalent interest rate that takes into account the level of risk involved (many sellers voluntarily agree to a somewhat lower rate, however). As with bank loans, there can be covenants about how the company uses its funds to make sure the loan obligation is honored before other possible expenses. In some cases, the seller may take a lower interest rate than would otherwise be the case in return for warrants representing the fair market value of the foregone interest. Warrants give the seller the right to buy X number of shares at the selling price for Y number of years into the future. They can be thought of as buying a stock option with the value of the foregone interest. When the warrants are exercised or come due, the company buys them back. Expert advice is needed to determine a fair value for the warrants, and trustees must determine the overall fairness of the transaction.

Many owners find seller notes especially attractive in environments where bank lending is restrictive and returns on alternative investments uncertain. The note itself can be an attractive investment, paying an interest rate above what could be achieved through bonds. At the same time, the seller is selling ownership and can reinvest the gains.

Company Cash Contributions

The company also can finance the acquisition by making tax-deductible discretionary cash contributions to the plan. These can be used to buy shares or can be held and invested until they reach a sufficient level to buy a target number of shares. The ESOP cannot hold only cash forever, however, without the IRS saying the plan is not an ESOP. Advisors generally say two or three years is fine, but more than that can raise issues.

Participation by Managers, Other Employees, or Outside Investors

In a few ESOPs, managers may put in some of their own money to buy shares, and/or outside investors can become buyers outside of the plan to provide needed equity. In these cases, financial advisors need to help structure the transaction so that these investors are treated fairly. It is also possible for these buyers to purchase equity interests other than stock, such as warrants. This may be done if the company wants to become 100% owned by the ESOP and convert to S status. As described later, this would allow the company to avoid paying federal and usually state income tax.

Even less commonly, employees can put some of their own money into the plan by moving assets from another plan (usually a 401(k) plan or profit sharing plan). The plan's fiduciary could unilaterally decide to move some portion of either employer- and/or employee-contributed assets into the ESOP, but this means moving money out of diversified investments into a single investment. If that investment does poorly, or even fails to do as well as a prudently created portfolio would, the fiduciary can be sued for misusing employee assets. To avoid this problem, some companies give employees a choice about whether to move their profit sharing funds into the ESOP, usually allowing them to move part or all of them. The first potential problem this creates is that not enough funds may be moved. The second is that the employees are making an investment decision in doing this. This will trigger securities law issues that can require expensive compliance. Most ESOP advisors, therefore, recommend that at most 15% to 30% of profit sharing assets be moved to an ESOP, and that the decision be made by the fiduciary with appropriate advice from independent financial experts. Even then, the funds should only be moved if there is good reason to believe the company's stock will be a good long-term investment relative to other investments. It is also safer to move only employer-contributed funds. Moving employee-contributed funds would likely trigger securities law issues, and the IRS has, to date, not looked favorably on this approach.

A separate chapter in this book provides more detail on financing issues.

How Much Can the ESOP Pay? The Annual Valuation Requirement

The sale to an ESOP is not like a normal negotiation between a buyer and a seller. The ESOP cannot pay more than fair market value. In a public company, this is determined by the market; in the much more common case of a closely held company, it must be determined by an independent, outside appraiser. The ESOP can pay less than fair market value. ESOP appraisals must be updated at least annually. This statutory requirement is necessary to provide appropriate pricing for repurchasing shares from employees, tax reporting, accounting, calculating the values in employee accounts, and many other purposes.[11] The appraiser should be hired by and work for the ESOP trust only and is required to provide a valuation based on the perspective of a financial buyer. The ESOP trustee must determine, based on this outside advice, whether the price is within the fair market value. "Independent" means that the appraiser can have no other business relationship with your company. Some companies hire an appraisal firm to do a preliminary valuation to determine whether the price the ESOP might pay is in an acceptable range, or to determine what can be financed. That firm is then hired by the trustee to do the appraisal for the ESOP. The Department of Labor has strongly indicated it believes the firm doing the preliminary valuation is conflicted if it stays on to be the valuation firm for the ESOP transaction, so either a new firm should be hired or the trustee should hire the appraiser at all phases of the transaction. The appraiser should have expertise and experience in ESOP valuations (the NCEO maintains a directory of these and other ESOP experts).

The ESOP appraiser determines what a willing third-party *financial* buyer would pay for the ownership being sold.[12] (See the chapter on valuation for details on the valuation process.) This distinction is important. A financial buyer determines what to pay based on the future free cash flow or earnings of the company and any marketable assets. A *synergistic* buyer, such as a competitor, may look at these same assets and earnings and offer more because of presumed synergies between the two companies that could enhance the combined earnings of the merged companies beyond what each of them separately would add up to. If this number is significantly higher than what the ESOP can pay, some sellers will be unwilling to go the ESOP route.

Because the valuation is so critical to the whole process, sellers who may be sensitive to the results should get a preliminary valuation before going much further in the ESOP process. For reasons detailed

---

11. See Code § 401(a)(28)(C) and Treas. Reg. § 54.4975-11(d)(5).

12. While no final regulations have ever been specifically issued for ESOP valuations, appraisers generally rely on the standards of value outlined in Revenue Rulings 59-60, 1959-1; 65-193, 1965-2, and 77-287, IRB 1977-33.

in the chapter on valuation, it is preferable that this be a different firm than the one ultimately doing the full-scale appraisal. This preliminary valuation will provide a brief report and a range of possible values.

Rules Relating to Participants

ESOPs have an exceptionally powerful set of tax incentives. In return for these incentives, companies must follow rules designed to make sure that the benefits of an ESOP are fairly allocated to employees, that the assets are protected from other competing interests, and that employees actually get their benefits.

The rules have eight basic parts: eligibility, allocations, vesting, diversification, distribution, the repurchase obligation, governance, and disclosure.

Eligibility

The rules for participation in an ESOP are largely the same as for other qualified employee benefit plans (pensions, profit sharing, etc.).[13] The rules provide several tests to assure plans meet minimum anti-discrimination requirements. Virtually all ESOP companies, however, cover at least all full-time employees (1,000 hours of service or more in a year) 21 years of age or older with at least one year of service. Employees covered by a collective bargaining agreement can be excluded from coverage, provided the company bargains in good faith about whether they should be included. These are minimum requirements; companies can include more employees (such as including part-time people or more recent hires).

The law does provide some additional exceptions. For example, the ESOP can include only employees in a separate line of business, such as a division or subsidiary, that has 50 or more employees. This will not apply, however, if the intent is to get around the coverage rules. For example, a plan could not just cover a division set up of management people and exclude a division that just has nonmanagement employees.

An alternative approach provides three tests for coverage. To use this approach, a company applies percentage tests to at least a mini-

---

13. Code § 401(a), particularly 401(a)(3), (4), (6), and (26), and Treas. Reg. § 1.401(a).

mum employee group. This group must include all employees age 21 or older who have completed at least 1,000 hours of service in a plan year, but it can exclude nonresident aliens, employees in a separate line of business with 50 or more employees, and employees covered by a collective bargaining agreement. After the exceptions have been taken, the tests can be met if:

1. At least 70% of non-highly compensated employees[14] are covered, or

2. The percentage of non-highly compensated employees who are covered is at least 70% of the percentage of highly compensated employees covered, or

3. There is a classification system that does not discriminate in favor of highly compensated employees, and the average benefit percentage (generally, the percentage of compensation contributed to all qualified retirement plans) for the covered non-highly compensated group is at least 70% of that contributed to the covered highly compensated group.

Although these alternative tests are available, they are very rarely used in ESOPs. The kind of exclusion the rules provide is both contrary to the spirit most ESOP companies are trying to set up and may cause practical problems if the effect of these formulas is to limit the eligible compensation in the ESOP to a number not large enough to support the needed annual contributions and/or annual additions to employee accounts.

Once an employee is eligible, there will be a plan entry date when that employee will join the plan. This could be once a year or more often.

---

14. A "highly compensated employee" is defined by Code Section 414(q)(1)(B) as someone who in the preceding year (1) owned more than 5% of the company or (2) received more than $120,000 in compensation (as of 2017; this figure is adjusted annually for inflation) and optionally was in the top 20% of employees ranked by compensation.

Allocations to Participants' ESOP Accounts

The ESOP cannot discriminate in favor of more highly compensated employees.[15] Most companies allocate stock based on compensation (typically defined as the amount on the employee's W-2 tax form), plus elective deferrals under Section 401(k) plans and cafeteria plans. That is, each participant in the plan gets a percentage of the total shares allocated equal to that participant's percentage of total eligible pay. Eligible pay excludes pay in excess of $270,000 per year as of 2017, as noted above. While W-2 compensation is the norm, compensation could also be defined to exclude bonuses or other "add-ons" to pay, provided the effect is not to push allocations toward more highly paid people. At least two-thirds of all ESOPs allocate on relative pay. Companies can create more level formulas, however, such as by lowering the maximum eligible pay or giving points for seniority. Any formula, however, needs a fail-safe provision that anyone who is a "highly compensated employee" (defined above under "Eligibility") cannot get more than what a relative pay formula would provide. In a non-leveraged ESOP, allocations are made when the contributions are made; in a leveraged ESOP, as noted above, shares are released as the loan is repaid.

If an employee leaves before being fully vested, any assets in that employee's accounts are reallocated to other employees based on the company's normal allocation formula.

Using Distributions or Dividends to Repay ESOP Loans

When C corporation dividends or S corporation distributions are used to repay an ESOP loan, the money put into the plan releases shares that have not yet been paid for, which are then allocated to employee accounts. Dividends or distributions that are paid on shares already allocated to employee accounts (those that have been paid for) release shares pro-rata to the percentage of shares held in each account; dividends or distributions paid on shares not already paid for can release shares to participant accounts based on relative account balances or on the company's usual allocation formula (most commonly, relative pay).

---

15. Code Section 401(a)(4); several safe harbors, such as relative pay, are set out in Treas. Reg. Section 1.401(a)(4)-2.

Dividends or distributions on allocated shares used to repay an ESOP loan must be used to release shares with a value at least equal to the dividend or distribution.[16] For example, say the ESOP has acquired 1,000 shares. After two years, 300 shares have been paid for and allocated to employee accounts. Mary's ESOP account has 5% of these shares (i.e., 15 shares), and she receives 4% of the company's eligible pay. A dividend is paid that is large enough to buy another 100 shares. Mary's account gets 5% of these additional shares (i.e., five shares) because her account had 5% of the previously allocated 300 shares. For the other 700 shares that are in the suspense account, Mary's account can either get another 5% (35 shares), based on her relative account balance (5% of the previously allocated 300 shares), or another 28 (4% of 700), based on her having 4% of the eligible pay. Most companies use the relative pay approach for unallocated shares to avoid a variety of potential problems beyond the scope of this discussion.

Vesting

Vesting must be 100% completed after three years of service with the company ("cliff vesting") or can start at not less than 20% after the second year of service and grow by at least another 20% per year until full vesting at 100% after six years. Vesting can be faster. Service before the ESOP can be counted (or not). A company could also give one year of vesting for every two years of prior service or some other formula, so long as it is applied to everyone.[17] If the plan is "top-heavy," meaning more than one third of the benefits go to highly compensated employees, faster vesting is required.[18]

Diversification

Plan participants must become eligible to diversify up to 25% of the shares in their account balances on the first day of the plan year following the end of the plan year in which they reach age 55 and have completed

---

16. Code § 404(k)(2)(B) (for C corporations); Code § 4975(f)(7) (for S corporations).

17. Code § 401(a)(17).

18. Code § 416.

10 years of participation in the plan.[19] At that point, the participant has 90 days to decide whether to diversify. For each of the next four years, at the start of the plan year, the employee has an additional 90-day period to elect to diversify. At the beginning of the sixth year, the percentage that can be diversified grows to a cumulative total of 50%. For the shares that employees choose to diversify, companies can pay out their value directly to the employee (where they would be subject to the put option described under the repurchase of shares), transfer the funds into a 401(k) or other qualified plan account the employee holds, or retain them in the ESOP and invest them in diversified assets.

Distributions

ESOP distribution rules are somewhat more complicated than rules for other defined contribution plans.[20] If an employee leaves because of death, retirement, or disability, distributions normally must start during the plan year following the plan year in which the event occurs, unless the participant elects otherwise. For all other cases, distribution must start within six years after the plan year of termination, unless the participant elects otherwise. Companies can always start distributions sooner. Companies need to have a written distribution policy. Ideally, these policies set the maximum times for distributions to begin, but allow some flexibility to be exercised in a nondiscriminatory fashion (the NCEO has sample policies).

However, if there is an outstanding ESOP loan, distributions to terminating employees do not have to start until the plan year after the plan year in which the loan is repaid.[21] There are certain exceptions to this for death and retirement, and the interaction of this rule with distributions made in installments is more complicated. The law applies this rule only to C corporations. While there is no logical reason why S corporations should not be able to condition distribution timing on the repayment, a literal reading of the law does not allow it.

In addition to the ESOP distribution rules given above, there are general rules that apply to all qualified plans. When there is a conflict

---

19. Code § 401(a)(28)(B).

20. Code § 401(a)(13) and (14).

21. Code §§ 409(o)(1)(B) and 401(a)(14).

between the ESOP distribution rules and the general distribution rules, the result that produces an earlier distribution applies. Under the general rules, distributions must start no later than the 60th day after the end of the plan year in which the later of these events occur: (1) the participant reaches age 65 or, if earlier, the plan's normal retirement age; (2) the participant's service terminates; or (3) the participant reaches the 10th anniversary of participation in the plan.

Once the distribution commences, it can be paid out in stock or in cash in a lump sum or in installments. S corporations and companies whose bylaws or charter require that all or substantially all the shares be held by the ESOP and/or employees can require the distribution to be in cash. The company and/or ESOP may maintain a right of first refusal on the shares. One installment option would be to pay out at least 20% or more of the total account each year. The value of the stock portion of the ESOP account and any invested other assets (by this point, there is often invested cash as well) would vary with the market, with the ESOP share value based on the most recent appraisal. Alternatively, the company can agree to pay for the value of the entire account at distribution at the then-current fair market value, but do so in installments with interest and adequate security in at least equal installments over five years. For very large distributions (as of 2017, balances over $1,080,000; this figure is indexed annually for inflation), one additional year can be added for installment payments for each additional one-fifth of that number.

Finally, a general retirement plan rule mandates that greater-than-5% owners who reach age 70½ and terminated employees who reach this age must start taking distributions no later than the April 1 after the calendar year in which they reach that age.

Repurchase of Shares

In closely held companies, when employees do receive a distribution in stock, they also receive a "put" right, meaning the company must repurchase the shares at fair market value.[22] The company can fund the ESOP to do this, but the ultimate obligation to make sure it happens rests with the company. If the shares are repurchased by the company, they can be retired or recontributed over time to the ESOP. Companies

---

22. Code § 409(h); Treas. Reg. § 54.4975-7(b)(10); DOL Reg. § 2550.408b-3(j).

have a right of first refusal on the shares, and S corporation ESOPs and companies whose bylaws require that all or substantially all the stock be owned by employees (in the ESOP or outside of it) can require that the employee actually take the fair market value of the shares in the distribution, not the shares themselves.

Some people have argued that this repurchase obligation means the company has to buy back its own stock twice. In fact, all closely held companies always have a 100% repurchase obligation all the time, no matter how often they or anyone else buys the shares. ESOPs pay this out in annual pieces, non-ESOP companies in periodic large chunks. The repurchase obligation is something ESOP companies need to plan for in advance, including doing projections of the obligation and having a plan to handle it.

Plan Governance

ESOPs are governed by a trustee appointed by the company's board. The trustee is normally either an outside institution with trust experience, most commonly a bank or trust company, an officer of the company, or a trust committee, usually made up of officers and/or employee representatives. The trustee normally is also the fiduciary—the person who is legally responsible for decisions concerning the plan. However, the board, a CEO, or anyone else who makes decisions for the plan, causes someone to make a decision about the plan, or, in some cases, provides misleading information to someone making decisions about the plan can also be a fiduciary. Put differently, it is anyone who exercises control over plan assets, directly or indirectly.

There are a number of fiduciary decisions. Setting up the plan, revising its rules, and terminating the plan, however, are notably not among them. Fiduciaries must act for the "exclusive benefit of plan participants,"[23] meaning when there is a conflict between participant and other interests, participant interests, as defined by their investment interest in the plan, must be favored. Specific fiduciary duties do include the following:

1. Buying and selling plan assets, including employer stock.

___
23. Code § 404(a)(1).

2. Hiring qualified advisors.

3. Determining that the ESOP is paying no more than fair market value.

4. Assuring that the plan is operated in accordance with plan documents and the Employee Retirement Income Security Act of 1974 (ERISA); if the two conflict, ERISA rules govern.

5. Making sure the terms of any ESOP loan are reasonable.

6. Voting and/or directing the tendering of shares in the trust for which the plan and the law do not require pass-through voting.

7. Deciding whether to follow participant voting or tendering directions on unallocated or undirected shares.

8. Responding to legitimate offers to purchase the company.

9. Acting to protect plan interests with respect to corporate actions that could harm the interests of plan participants.

The trustee decides how to vote the shares, including voting for who is on the board, most of the time. The law does require, however, that voting rights in closely held companies must be passed through on all allocated shares (vested or not) to plan participants on their allocated shares for certain limited issues, most importantly the sale of all or substantially all the assets of the company (but not the stock), mergers, and recapitalization of stock. In most ESOP companies, there is never a required vote pass-through. Companies can voluntarily pass through greater voting rights.[24] In public companies, participants must be able to direct the voting of their shares on any issues put to shareholder vote.

Disclosures and Benefit Statements

ESOP companies have only limited disclosure requirements. When a plan is first adopted, participants must be notified before the end of the first plan year that a new plan is in place. Plan participants also must get a summary plan description describing the rules of the plan and rights of participants. They must have an ongoing right to inspect the plan document. On an ongoing basis, the most basic disclosure requirement

---

24. Code § 409(e).

is to provide a statement of benefits to participants. The statement must include at least a statement of the participant's accrued benefit (account balances in a defined contribution plan such as an ESOP), a statement of vested benefits and/or a statement of when benefits will become vested, and a description of the information used to compute benefit accruals. The administrator must also furnish a summary annual report (SAR) each year to all participants or beneficiaries receiving benefits under the plan. The SAR is a very abbreviated summary of the activity of the plan and must be presented in a form provided by the Department of Labor regulations. When employees are eligible to diversify shares or get distributions, employers must provide them with appropriate notifications and explanations.

Note that none of this requires the disclosure of any kind of financial information about the company (income statements, salaries, the valuation report, etc.), board minutes, government filings other than the Form 5500 report on plan participation and assets (and then only if the participant requests it), etc. The disclosure rules for ESOPs are essentially parallel to those for any other kind of retirement plan. Effective ESOP companies, however, voluntarily choose to share a great deal of information on corporate performance, although almost never on salaries.

S Corporation Issues

ESOPs in S corporations have a particular and powerful tax advantage. While it might seem that these advantages would only apply to smaller companies because of the 100-owner limitation for S corporations, the ESOP actually counts as one shareholder, no matter how many participants there are. A principal difference in tax benefits is that sellers to an ESOP in an S corporation, however, cannot get a tax deferral on their gains from the sale. Moreover, when the ESOP is leveraged, interest and principal payments on the loan count toward the contribution limits.

On the other hand, earnings attributable to the ESOP are not taxable.[25] What literally happens is that the ESOP gets a Schedule K-1 like any other shareholder. But its tax rate is zero, so it pays no tax on the

---

25. The provision allowing an ESOP to be an S corporation shareholder is Code Section 1361(c)(6); the provision exempting the ESOP from taxable obligation on company profits is Code Section 512(e)(3).

income attributable to it. So if an ESOP owns 30% of an S corporation's stock, 30% of its profits are effectively not subject to federal, and, almost always, state income tax. In a 100% ESOP, this means no income tax is due. As a result, many S corporations with ESOPs are 100% ESOP-owned.

If an S corporation makes distributions to its owners so that they can pay their taxes (or for any other reason), the ESOP still must get a pro-rata share. This is an S corporation requirement, not an ESOP requirement. These distributions are allocated to employee accounts based on each participant's relative share of the total shares in the ESOP for shares that have been allocated. For shares still held in a suspense account in a leveraged ESOP, the distributions can attach in the same way or be allocated based on the normal allocation formula. In 100% ESOPs, there is no need to make distributions because the owner—the ESOP trust—pays no taxes. As a result, it is very rare for these companies to make distributions, instead retaining the money for other purposes.

If a company does convert from C to S status, usually after an ESOP sale, it is subject to built-in gains taxes for 10 years. These are taxes due on appreciated assets should the company be sold. If an S corporation converts to C status before an ESOP sale, usually to afford the owners the opportunity to take the Section 1042 tax deferral, it cannot convert back to S status for five years.

Whether to convert to C status before setting up an ESOP depends on several factors, primarily (but not exclusively) including the basis of the seller's shares (in some S corporations where sellers have been paying their own taxes and not taking distributions, the basis may be very high) and whether there are other non-selling owners who want to retain the S status.

The ability to avoid taxes predictably drew scam artists who tried to design ESOPs in a way that their benefits could be captured by just a few people in a company or for sole proprietors, partners, or other owners of small businesses with no employees. Just as predictably, the IRS and Congress cracked down. The result was a set of "anti-abuse" rules for S corporation ESOPs.[26] These are far from perfect—they catch some very small companies that really do want to share ownership broadly.

---

26. Code § 409(p) and Treas. Reg. § 1.409(p)-IT.

Most of these are very small (15 employees or fewer typically), but they can catch larger companies that do not structure their plans properly.

The rules have two steps:

1. First, determine who as an individual owns 10% or more, or as part of a family owns 20% or more, of the "deemed-owned shares." Deemed-owned shares are (1) shares allocated to an individual in the ESOP, (2) the individual's pro-rata share of unallocated ESOP stock, and (3) any claims on ownership (such as stock options, restricted stock, phantom stock, stock appreciation rights, and certain deferred compensation arrangements). These claims on ownership such as stock options are called "synthetic equity," that is, benefits that have some of the attributes of real ownership but are not actually direct ownership. Anyone is this group is considered a "disqualified person." Family members include spouses, lineal ascendants or descendants, siblings and their children, and the spouses of any of these family members.

2. Second, determine whether disqualified persons own at least 50% of all shares in the company. In making this determination, ownership is defined to include:

    a. shares held directly (in contrast with step 1 above)

    b. shares owned through synthetic equity, including the equivalent equity value of any deferred compensation paid out after more than 2.5 months after the compensation award is granted

    c. shares allocated to the individual's ESOP account

    d. the individual's pro-rata share of the unallocated shares owned through the ESOP

If disqualified individuals own (or are deemed to own) at least 50% of the stock of the company, then the company has a "nonallocation year" and is subject to penalties. In the first nonallocation year, there is a 50% tax on the fair market value of shares allocated to all disqualified individuals even if no additional allocations are made to those individuals that year (in other words, the tax applies simply if disqualified individuals own, or are deemed to own, more than 50% of the company in the first year).

In addition, disqualified persons may not receive allocations from the ESOP during nonallocation years without a substantial tax penalty. If such an allocation does occur, it is taxed as a distribution to the recipient and a 50% corporate excise tax would apply to the fair market value of the stock allocated. If synthetic equity is owned, a 50% excise tax would also apply to its value as well.

Finally, both an allocation to a disqualified person and the accumulation of ownership or deemed ownership of 50% or more of the stock constitute a prohibited allocation, and the plan would no longer be an ESOP.

These rules may seem dauntingly complex, but if your company has more than 15 employees (and possibly as few as 10), good plan design can prevent these events from happening. In the worst case, if they are about to happen and cannot be avoided, a company can just convert to C status.

Reinvesting the "Rollover" on a Section 1042 Tax-Deferred Sale

As explained above under "Tax Benefits," owners who sell to a C corporation ESOP and qualify under the rules described above for the Section 1042 tax-deferred treatment must invest ("roll over") in "qualified replacement property" (QRP) to receive the deferral. (A separate chapter of this book discusses this issue in detail, so only the basics of investing in QRP are described here.)

QRP consists of stocks, bonds, debentures, warrants, or other debt or equity instruments issued by U.S. operating corporations that receive not more than 25% of their income from passive investments (that is, from income from investments in other things than their own business). U.S. companies are companies controlled by U.S. firms, not simply companies with operating units in the U.S. and listed on U.S. stock exchanges (Schlumberger or Food Lion, for example, would be foreign firms). Mutual funds, U.S. government bonds, and municipal bonds, for example, do not qualify. Securities of banks and insurance companies are specifically designated as "operating corporations" that qualify as QRP. The company whose securities are purchased as QRP can be public or private and can be owned by the seller to the ESOP. It cannot be owned by the company sponsoring the ESOP, however.

The seller must purchase QRP within the 15-month period starting 3 months before the sale and ending 12 months afterward. The seller must obtain a notarized statement of purchase indicating which securities have been purchased within 30 days after the securities are purchased. In addition, the seller must file an irrevocable statement of election on or before the tax return due date for the tax year in which the sale occurs. This election must describe the securities sold to the ESOP, the sale date, the adjusted basis of the shares, the amount for which they sold, the identity of the ESOP that purchased the shares, and information about the sale of securities to other parties than the ESOP if the sale was part of a larger transaction. Finally, there must be a statement of consent by the company to the election. These forms are not available from the government, but most brokerage firms, ESOP advisors, or law firms handling the Section 1042 transaction will have their own version of the forms.

The seller pays no tax on the gains from the sale to the ESOP until any of these new investments are sold, at which point the basis would be the original basis of the owner in his or her company. The basis held in QRP until death would be stepped up at that time. The seller could also donate QRP to a charity at the full value, not the value after tax. This means the charity gets more and the owner gets a bigger tax deduction.

For most people, advisors tell us the ideal QRP portfolio would consist of 30 to 50 or so investments of varying risk, all of which are designed to be long-term holds (albeit you can always sell any part and pay the tax). Bonds should be noncallable because once called, tax is due.

If a seller loans to an ESOP, the rollover is a little more complicated. The reinvestment of gains has to occur during the 15-month window described above. If the seller has that much cash available from the first installment payment and other sources, this can all be used—the IRS does not track the source of the reinvestment funds. But if the seller is using only the installment payments, after the 12-month post-sale period, further installments would not be eligible. To resolve this issue, there are now special "ESOP Notes." These are variable-rate, very long-term, noncallable bonds that the seller can borrow money from a lender to buy (usually with a 10% or 20% down payment). These qualify as QRP. As the loan to buy the QRP is repaid, the seller can, if desired, use that to margin other investments.

Some sellers will choose simply not to take the rollover, however, even if they qualify. Some people believe tax rates will go up eventually, so it is better to pay the tax now (most advisors I have talked to say the math on this rarely works out, however). Others may prefer to invest in things that do not qualify as QRP, such as government bonds or mutual funds. Still other sellers may wish to avoid taking the rollover so they or others who would be excluded under Section 1042 (certain relatives and more-than-25% owners) can participate in the ESOP if they work for the company.

Steps to Setting Up an ESOP

If you have decided an ESOP is worth investigating, there are several steps to take to implement a plan. At each point, you may decide you have gone far enough and that an ESOP is not right for you.

1. Get Educated

The more you know about ESOPs, the better you will be able to control the process at every step and not have to rely solely on what advisors tell you. The NCEO has a variety of ways to do this, including seminars, webinars, an annual conference, this and other publications, and, for members, the right to call or email us at any time for advice. We also can refer members to ESOP company leaders to talk to.

2. Determine Whether Owners Really Are Willing to Sell to an ESOP or Would Rather Try to Find Another Buyer

Seller reticence can come up in a number of ways. The first is whether company owners are primarily interested in getting the highest price possible. An ESOP may offer that, especially if the owner figures in potential tax benefits, but, as noted earlier, in some cases there may be one or more synergistic buyers out there who could offer an even better deal (or at least one or more owners perceives this to be the case). A second barrier can be that the company's culture just is not the right fit. If one or more owners just don't like the idea of employees becoming owners "for free," or they really only want to give ownership to certain people, or they cannot imagine ever doing any of the kinds of ownership culture things that make ESOP companies really successful, as discussed toward the end of this chapter, then implementing an ESOP may not be the best thing to do.

4. Have a Preliminary Valuation Performed

You may want to have a preliminary valuation done first to see whether the range of values produced is acceptable. Even if you are determined to proceed with an ESOP at a lower price, however, the data from the valuation will allow you to assess more specifically how much money is needed to fund the plan.

4. Conduct a Feasibility Study

This may be a full-blown analysis by an outside consultant, replete with market surveys, management interviews, and detailed financial projections, or it may simply be a careful business plan created in-house. Generally, full-scale feasibility studies are needed only where there is some doubt about the ESOP's ability to repay the loan. Any analysis, however, must look at several items. First, it must assess just how much extra cash flow the company has available to devote to the ESOP, and whether this is adequate for the purposes for which the ESOP is intended. Second, it must determine whether the company's eligible payroll is large enough so that contributions within the annual limits can repay the ESOP loan in a reasonable time or, in, a non-leveraged purchase, will buy enough stock each year to satisfy the sellers (note, however, that this is very rarely a problem). Remember to include the effect of other benefit plans that will be maintained in these calculations. Third, estimates must be made of what the repurchase obligation will be and how the company will handle it. Finally, it must make a preliminary assessment of how the ESOP will be financed (seller financing, outside financing, ongoing cash contributions, etc.) and whether this financing is available.

5. Hire an ESOP Attorney

If these first steps prove positive, the plan can now be drafted and submitted to the IRS. You should carefully evaluate your options and tell your attorney just how you want the ESOP to be set up. This could save you a considerable amount of money in consultation time. The IRS may take many months to issue you a "letter of determination" on your plan, but you can go ahead and start making contributions before then. If the IRS rules unfavorably, which rarely happens, normally you just need to amend your plan.

In locating an attorney or any other ESOP professional, keep in mind that many people will claim to have expertise in this area, but relatively few actually do. The NCEO maintains a service provider directory on its website to help people find providers (we do not endorse these providers, however). You should interview at least three professionals in each area and ask each one for a list of prior ESOP engagements. Look for evidence of involvement in ESOP organizations, speaking and writing on the topic, and referrals from ESOP clients.

6. Arrange Financing

We have already discussed the various means to finance a plan. Remember, these can be combined. If enough financing cannot be found to buy all the stock that is for sale, consider doing a smaller purchase in the first round and buying more later.

7. Establish a Process to Operate the Plan

A trustee must be chosen to oversee the plan. A process should be set up, preferably with employee involvement, to communicate the new plan to employees. Finally, to be really effective, a process should be set up to find ways to get employees more involved as owners by making it easier for them to share ideas and information.

Creating an Ownership Culture

You can set up an ESOP just as a benefit plan with no implications for corporate culture, but the research is definitive that companies that create (or already have) what we call an "ownership culture" vastly outperform those that do not. Starting in the 1980s, study after study has shown that employees generally like being owners. The more shares they own, the more committed they are to their company, the more satisfied they are with their jobs, and the less likely they are to leave.

The size of the company, line of business, demographic characteristics of the employees, seniority, job classification, presence or absence of voting rights or board membership, percentage of the company owned by employees (as opposed to the size of the annual contribution), and many other factors do not have any impact on these attitudes.

But job satisfaction and even motivation do not automatically translate into performance. The key is not just for employees to like what they do, and do it more carefully or energetically (both of which can make a small difference in overall company performance, but only a small one, it turns out), but to be able, as owners, to contribute better ideas and information on how the company can make more money. The companies that make this happen, the research shows, have three characteristics:

1. They regularly share information about how the company is doing overall, and they break it down into measurements and goals at the work level.

2. They provide structured opportunities for employees to share ideas and information, such as teams, ad-hoc committees, defining jobs to give individuals more individual authority, and company-wide and/or other functional unit meetings. Just having an "open-door" policy is far from enough (virtually every company has an open-door policy, we have found).

3. They provide training for employees on ownership and participation issues, including extensive communications about how the plan works.

The structure of participation varies from firm to firm, but basically boils down to employees forming groups to share information, generate ideas, and make recommendations.

At Phelps County Bank in Rolla, Missouri, the ESOP was at first a sleepy benefit plan. Then Emma Lou Brent, the bank's CEO, read that for an ESOP to work, employees must receive substantial annual contributions and have a chance to share their ideas and information on a regular basis. So Brent increased the ESOP contribution to 25% of pay per year and started an employee involvement program based on a "problem-buster committee." Employees formed a committee to solicit input on what issues were causing difficulties. Brightly colored "problem alerts" were then circulated to ask for ideas on how to solve them. Often, the solution was to form an ad hoc team of people who thought they had something to contribute. The system has grown over the years and now includes extensive training in bank management for all employees. The result is that the company's stock has gone up much faster than the increase in costs; in fact, Phelps has been one of the best-performing banks in its class for years, and employees typically leave with accounts in the mid-six figures.

At Springfield ReManufacturing in Springfield, Missouri, employee owners are taught to read detailed financial and production data. Meeting in work groups, they go over the numbers and then figure out ways to improve them. Employees are given monthly 110-page financial statements to digest. A waste of time? Springfield's stock went from 10 cents a share when it started its ESOP in the early 1980s to over $435 in a recent (2015) valuation. Employment is up from 130 to 1,400.

Other approaches include employee advisory committees to management, eliminating levels of supervision while giving nonmanagement employees more authority, meetings between management and randomly selected groups of employees, suggestion boxes, and anything else companies can imagine to get people involved.

None of this is easy to do, but the results consistently have demonstrated the worth of the effort. As a result, participative management has become the hottest topic in ESOPs. Not a conference goes by without repeated imprecations, from consultants and experienced companies alike, to get moving in this area.

Best Practices for Implementing an ESOP

ESOPs must comply with a variety of rules, but there still is considerable flexibility in how they can be designed. Below are several of the most common options that people can overlook.

You can share ownership outside the ESOP in a variety of ways: If you want specific people to buy into the plan beyond what they would get in the ESOP, you can have them buy shares at fair market value or a discount (the discount is taxable). The company can loan them the money, or they can purchase shares out of future bonuses. You can put a restriction on these shares so that they cannot take possession of them until they meet certain performance and/or seniority targets (these shares are called "restricted stock"). You can also make outright grants of shares, again with the options on restricting the right to take possession until they fully vest based on seniority, performance, or both. You can give employees stock options, phantom stock, or stock appreciation rights. If you do not want them to own actual shares, phantom stock and stock appreciation rights would work, as would warrants with a mandatory redemption feature before exercise. If you do grant equity (as opposed to having it purchased), it should be in line with what can be justified by individual performance. Excessive grants can raise issues with the ESOP.

You can structure the ESOP loan over a longer period of time than the company loan: I mentioned earlier that the loan to the ESOP can be longer than the loan to the company to buy the shares. As noted above, this can help you stay within contribution limits or function to spread benefits more gradually over time. Many ESOPs have a five- to seven-year loan. If all the stock is allocated over this time, what happens as new employees come on board? If any shares are repurchased or reallocated, they can get some of those, but their ESOP contributions would be very limited. Usually, at that point, companies start putting in cash contributions to the plan unless there are more shares to buy, leaving new employees with few shares and mostly cash, and senior employees with the opposite. A longer internal loan schedule will spread out the share release more. There are no specific limits on just how long this can be, but the effect should not be to make the needed annual contributions below a fairly robust level (I would suggest at least 7% or 8% of pay). Also, there should be a provision to start paying people out after a reasonable time even if the loan is not fully repaid (10 years seems reasonable).

Your distribution policy can be flexible: While you should make it possible to pay people out as late as the law requires, a good distribution policy will have a provision providing for faster distributions if cash is available. The policy must be carefully written to make sure it is nondiscriminatory and meets various other rules, but this is a common ap-proach. Waiting the maximum time to make distributions is not always a good idea, such as when the stock value is rising faster than your cost of money or you would rather not have former employees benefitting from stock value increases. You can also "segregate" accounts of former employees by buying out their shares, but not paying them out the cash that is reinvested in the plan until later. That means former employees don't benefit from (or take the risk of) holding stock, but do not have the incentive to terminate an immediate payout might provide.

Take ownership culture seriously: It is easy to get wrapped up in all the technical and financial issues of an ESOP and put off communications and culture until later. But the sooner you get started on these issues, the better off you are. If the culture does not support the notion of employees as owners, eventually the employees may become cynical about the ESOP, even if it is a good benefit.

Explain, don't sell: When you do tell employees about the ESOP, try not to make it a sale pitch. Explain the benefits and the risks, as well as what is in it for sellers and the company. We have found employees are much more responsive to this approach. Over time, if the ESOP is successful, then it is time to celebrate.

Call us: The NCEO does not set up plans, but our staff has a great deal of experience in the area. If you are an NCEO member, we can give you objective feedback on any issue you are likely to face.

Be patient: The process will take time and more of your involvement than other ways to sell a company usually do. ESOPs are not for everyone, but if they work for you, the investment is well worthwhile.

Conclusion

Employee ownership is not the right solution for every business owner seeking to sell. There are a great many owners of closely held companies, however, for whom it is a great solution, but who either do not know about the plan or whose advisors tell them all sorts of things that are not true, whether out of ignorance or a fear of losing a client because the advisor does not handle ESOPs. Many sellers to ESOPs would tell you that the ESOP was just what they were looking for. They get a fair price, good tax benefits, and the satisfaction of knowing they did the right thing.

Chapter 2

Should You Sell to an ESOP?

Loren Rodgers and Corey Rosen

About 7,000 companies in the United States have ESOPs. These plans include almost 14 million participants. ESOP companies range from those as small as Union Fish, with just five employees, to companies with over 100,000 employees. The data show that for almost all these companies, the decision to become an ESOP worked well for owners, employees, communities, and companies. Of course, many more companies have *not* adopted ESOPs. Some business owners have excellent reasons: they may want to retain 100% ownership themselves, or they may have researched ESOPs and decided that they were not a good fit. For too many, however, ESOPs are not on the table because the owners believe one of the common myths about ESOPs, or perhaps they are simply unaware that ESOPs exist.

This chapter briefly describes the potential benefits and disadvantages of ESOPs, then covers some "easy no" examples—situations where an ESOP is unambiguously a bad fit. Sales to an outsider and management buyouts are the two most common alternatives to ESOPs, so we consider the advantages and disadvantages of each relative to ESOPs, first in general and then by using a case study with multiple scenarios. Next, we examine the differences between partial and 100% ESOP transactions. The chapter closes by debunking some common myths and listing the key decision points for people considering an ESOP.

Advantages of ESOPs

Much of what you will read and hear about ESOPs, including this book, talks about the tax and financing advantages of ESOPs. But for Ken Baker, CEO of New Age Industries, an ESOP-owned manufacturer in

Pennsylvania, that misses the point. For Baker, the decision was much more about legacy, community, and employees. He wanted to make the transition out of ownership over time so he could stay with the company as long as he wants, so that the employees who helped him build the business could become the owners of New Age and not the employees of another buyer (or even lose their jobs), to give employees a reason to care about the success of the company, and keep the company a contributing part of the community. Selling to another buyer just seemed wrong.

Most business owners who think about ESOPs we have talked to feel the same way, although it's certainly not a requirement to be a good ESOP candidate. But as readers go through the tax and financial issues involved with the ESOP decision, Baker's reminder that there is more to business transition than money is worth remembering.

The good news for owners who do want to sell to an ESOP, and whose companies are the right fit, is that good intentions can be rewarded with significant financial advantages:

Tax deferral of capital gains: When owners of C corporation shares meet specific requirements in connection with selling their shares to an ESOP, they may defer capital gains taxes and possibly avoid them entirely if the qualified replacement property they buy with the proceeds of the ESOP sale becomes part of their estate.

Partial sales: Most private investors are not willing to buy partial stakes in private companies, while an ESOP is well suited to a partial sale or a series of sales that culminate in the original owner selling his or her entire ownership interest.

Using pretax dollars: ESOPs are the only way the company can use *pretax dollars* to buy out current owners. If a company buys shares back from an owner outside of an ESOP, it will need to use after-tax dollars. Any buyer other than the company will also be using cash on which tax has already been paid, effectively increasing the cost to the buyer. If a seller will be retaining partial ownership of the company, this tax benefit will increase the value of his or her remaining shares. In many cases, the ESOP sale will yield a comparable or better after-tax return than other sales, especially when all contingencies are considered.

Income tax shield: When an S corporation sponsors an ESOP, a portion of its income is no longer subject to federal income tax. So if an owner of an S corporation sells part of the ownership to an ESOP, the company will pay lower taxes going forward, enhancing future profits. A 100% ESOP-owned S corporation pays no federal income tax, so if an S corporation becomes 100% ESOP-owned and the sale to the ESOP is seller-financed, the seller's likelihood of repayment will be higher than in the case of a 100% sale to an ESOP in an equivalent C corporation.

Timing: An ESOP allows sellers to sell at their own pace, retaining whatever role they prefer in the company. That may mean sellers stay on as managers, consultants, and/or board members indefinitely or they may gradually withdraw to a more limited role. Other owners leave day-to-day management immediately after selling shares to an ESOP. While it is possible for other transaction structures to allow flexible timing, it is not typical and generally the subject of difficult negotiations.

Work force: ESOPs tend to improve employees' retirement assets significantly. Moreover, while other buyers often reduce employment, there is no reason that needs to happen when an ESOP becomes the owner.

Compensation flexibility: ESOPs allow companies to grant or sell equity to individual employees outside the ESOP. In non-100% ESOP-owned companies this equity may be simply stock, or it can be stock appreciation rights, phantom stock, or other forms of equity-linked or equity-based compensation in any company.

Resistance to offers: ESOP companies can be sold down the road just like any other company, but ESOP companies are difficult to purchase if they do not want to be sold.

Improved performance: ESOP companies have, on average, better productivity, faster sales growth, and faster employment growth.

Work environment: ESOP companies have a unique advantage in creating organizational cultures that are fulfilling and highly engaging. Anonymous respondents in employee surveys the NCEO has administered in ESOP companies describe employee ownership as "the American dream," "the kind of company I have always wanted to work for," and "the way it ought to be."

Disadvantages of ESOPs

Even in companies where ESOPs are appropriate, they do impose some burdens.

Setup and operational expenses: The company must pay legal costs to set up the plan and to keep it current and compliant. Administrative costs include both the expense associated with an outside administration firm and the cost in staff time of monitoring the administration firm and providing it with the necessary data. Before the ESOP transaction and annually thereafter, the company must pay for an independent valuation of its stock. An ESOP will probably cost $75,000 to $150,000 or more to set up and run the first year and, for most companies with under a few hundred people, about $25,000–$35,000 annually if they have internal trustees and about $20,000 more if they have external trustees. These costs are typically lower than the costs of selling to another company, however, and the tax benefits of an ESOP on an ongoing basis are far larger than the costs.

Demands on cash: The vast majority of companies contribute more to their ESOPs than they would have contributed to retirement plans without an ESOP. When there is an ESOP loan, the company will have little if any flexibility in terms of reducing this demand on cash or managing the timing of payments. Companies are also responsible for repurchasing shares from former participants, which often amounts to buying back 2% to 5% of shares yearly in mature ESOP companies.

Regulatory scrutiny: Both the IRS and the Department of Labor may investigate ESOPs, causing a burden in the demands they make and a risk of penalties or costly measures to cure any defects they may find.

Purchase price: The ESOP will pay fair market value for shares based on what a financial buyer would pay, but it will not be able to match a synergistic price that a strategic buyer might offer.

Fiduciary risk: The trustee of the ESOP is held to strict standards of fiduciary responsibility, which may impose costs on the company in the form of insurance for fiduciaries or litigation by unhappy plan participants. The risk may be borne by an inside trustee (often a company officer) or an outside fee-based trustee. While successful litigation by plan participants is rare, companies need to understand their exposure and take steps to minimize risk.

Lack of flexibility: While ESOPs are flexible in many ways, they are subject to legal constraints. ESOP rules require that contributions be allocated based on relative compensation (counting amounts up to $270,000 as of 2017; this figure is indexed annually for inflation) or some more level formula. Moreover, everyone who has worked for 1,000 hours in a 12-month period must be in the plan (with certain exceptions, such as employees covered by a collective bargaining agreement). The ESOP rules do not allow companies to direct allocations within the plan to reward specific employees.

When ESOPs Are Clearly Not the Right Choice

Given the competing advantages and disadvantages, some companies will require financial modeling by an expert to determine whether an ESOP is viable. In some circumstances, though, a simple preliminary checklist can identify a company as a bad candidate for an ESOP. Some situations in which an ESOP is highly unlikely to be a good fit are listed below.

ESOPs are usually impractical for very small companies (typically under 10 to 15 employees): First, implementation costs may be greater than potential tax benefits. Second, if the company is an S corporation, anti-abuse rules aimed at preventing a small number of people from getting the bulk of the ESOP benefits may make an ESOP impossible even if all employees are in the plan. The company could convert to C status, however.

The current owner's primary concern is to maximize his or her proceeds from the sale, and a strategic buyer is willing to offer a substantial premium: This is a common and valid reason for a company to choose not to adopt an ESOP, but a strategic sale does not work in all circumstances. For example, if a company has multiple owners, all must be looking to get out entirely. Where there is a single owner, that owner may only want to sell part of his or her ownership. In addition, the strategic buyer's premium must be large enough to offset the ability of a seller to a qualifying ESOP to defer taxation on the gain by reinvesting in other securities under Section 1042 of the Internal Revenue Code. Last, the buyer's offer must not contain unacceptable contingencies or uncertain financing.

The company lacks reliable cash flow: When an ESOP is buying out an owner, the cost is a non-productive expense. Companies need to assess whether they have the available earnings for this. ESOPs are not usually good choices for struggling companies and are often difficult in companies that experience wide year-to-year swings in earnings.

Capable successor management is not in place: Especially when the seller is a key manager, committed management is necessary to obtain an outside loan as well as to help assure that the company will be able to pay for the plan over time.

The company is not a C or S corporation: LLCs, partnerships, and other such forms of business cannot adopt ESOPs without first converting to C or S corporation status.

Family members or executives want a major share of the company: As discussed above, an ESOP cannot be used to transfer ownership to specific people. Additionally, when a seller to an ESOP elects the Section 1042 tax deferral, the seller, certain family members of the seller, and more-than-25% owners cannot receive ESOP allocations of any shares from the Section 1042 transaction. Individuals can buy or, within reasonable limits, be given shares outside the ESOP, or be given equity rights such as stock options or stock appreciation rights. If the goal is to transfer most of the ownership to a select group, then an ESOP is not appropriate.

Companies to which none of the above apply may want to explore the feasibility of an ESOP. Whether an ESOP is the best option for a company or not depends on what the other alternatives are, so the next sections of this chapter explore sales to outsiders and management buyouts.

Sales to Outsiders

Outsiders could be anyone not employed at the company: a private equity firm, another business, or a non-employee member of the owner's family. These outside buyers will often be strategic buyers, who believe that the company is worth more after they buy it than it is worth on its own. Such strategic buyers are willing to pay a higher price than a financial buyer (who is looking only at the present value of the company's projected earnings), and the strategic premium can be substantial. The ESOP will pay what an appraiser determines a financial buyer would pay (such as an individual investor or private equity company), so in the event that price is the primary criteria and a solid offer exists, an ESOP may not be the owner's best option.

Still, in financial terms, the ESOP may be more competitive than it appears at first glance. It often pays cash, while outside buyers often pay partly in cash and partly in an earnout. (In a number of cases, however, ESOPs are seller financed, meaning that the seller receives a note instead of or in addition to cash as payment for his or her shares.) Other buyers also cannot offer the opportunity the ESOP does for the seller to defer capital gains tax on the sale. The combined federal and state tax burden can range from 20% to, in California, 33.8% of the value of the sale.

The costs associated with a non-ESOP sale can also be high. Selling to another company usually involves some tens of thousands of dollars in legal, accounting, and valuation fees, plus, if there is a broker (as there often is), another 3% to 5% or more of the transaction. There is no broker in an ESOP. So for most sellers of all but the smallest companies, an ESOP is actually cheaper than selling some other way. Setup fees can be more in some cases, depending on financing sources and whether independent fiduciaries are required.

Occasionally, an ESOP may cost much more to set up, but this is almost always only in those cases where an investment banker is helping to secure financing through private placement of debt. If someone tells you an ESOP should cost hundreds of thousands of dollars just for legal, administrative, and appraisal costs, find someone else.

The ESOP also has some non-financial advantages that may make it a more comfortable fit for the current owner. First, most unsolicited offers are not credible. Many are "fishing," where the potential buyer is not knowledgeable about the field. Second, strategic buyers often have other relationships with the company. They may be vendors, competitors, or customers, making the company reluctant to share the financial information required for the deal's due diligence. Third, many sellers want to sell out gradually, or there may be just one owner who wants to sell now while others want to wait. Private investors and other companies will not buy partial ownership interests except in unusual cases. Fourth, there may also be personal contingencies on the sale, such as requiring the seller to stay (or to leave). Last, outside buyers often replace key employees or even all the employees and may relocate or rename the firm. For many owners, preserving the legacy of the company they built is important.

Thinking back on his decision to sell his company, Windings, to an ESOP, Roger Ryberg acknowledges that he could have taken home more money for his shares. He says, "Other objectives were more important to me. I know that people with bigger pots of money aren't necessarily as fulfilled as I am."

Management Buyouts

Rather than an outsider, another common consideration is whether it would be better for managers to buy the company directly. From the seller's perspective, this may be a way to transfer ownership to a select and preferred group of people. The tax treatment, from the seller's perspective, would be similar to that described for a sale to outsiders, including the ability to structure the sale so that the seller would be taxed at capital gains rates (although, unlike an ESOP, there is no possibility that the tax can be deferred).

The trick comes in financing the sale. There are a number of ways to structure such a sale, most often by the seller taking a note from the individuals making the purchase. The buyers have to repay this note entirely out of after-tax earnings, however, whereas an ESOP uses pre-tax earnings. To make the payments at least partly deductible, it is also common for some of the sale price to be paid in the form of a consulting fee, board fees, the leasing of hard assets or intellectual property, and so on. While this saves the buyers tax dollars, it means the seller now must declare ordinary income on any of these payments.

From the management side, it might seem at first blush that management simply purchasing the company outright would provide them with the greatest long-term financial return. While an ESOP is highly tax-favored, management would only get a portion of the ownership based on strict ESOP allocation rules. The comparison between the two models, however, is not that simple, in part because a management buyout requires the managers to invest their own capital, often by taking on personal debt, while their gain in an ESOP is a company contribution. As a result, managers are often better off being participants in an ESOP buyout than buying the whole company themselves, even if they have the funds to make the purchase (which they usually don't).

Case Study

We can illustrate these alternatives with a hypothetical example. Joe Murphy wants to sell Midwest Services Company (MSC) to his managers. He founded the company 30 years ago and owns all of its shares. The business is worth $5 million and has 50 employees. Its revenue and earnings have been solid, and the company projects continued growth over the next seven years. The five-person management team is talented and has an average of 12 years of service at MSC.

Scenario 1: Sale to an Outsider

After ignoring unsolicited offers for years, Joe decided it was time to take a closer look. The first several offers that came to him were clearly form letters, which he discarded. Then he took a call from the CFO of ServCorp, one of MSC's vendors, which is a much larger company with national sales and a sterling reputation. Joe knew the ServCorp's CFO from trade shows and sales visits. The CFO outlined an offer of $3 million in cash, $2 million in a four-year note that would be paid if earnings targets were met, and $2 million in ServCorp stock.

Joe founded MSC, so his basis in the shares was zero. He would pay capital gains taxes on the $7 million proceeds from the sale. Assuming a combined federal and state capital gains rate of 25%, he would pay 25% in taxes on the $3 million in cash from the sale. If the $2 million note is properly structured, he would pay 25% of $2 million in capital gains over the four-year period, plus tax on the interest. The ServCorp stock received in exchange would not be taxable until it was sold, at which time it would also be taxed as a capital gain, with the basis being Joe's basis in the MSC shares. Ignoring the potential gain or loss in ServCorp's stock, Joe would net $5.25 million on the value of the stock sold.

A friend of Joe's who had recently sold his company suggested some questions Joe might want to ask about ServCorp and its plans. He also recommended that Joe do some research on ServCorp and hire a financial advisor and a lawyer to ensure that the deal was in his best interests. The friend's questions made Joe think about all the nonfinancial aspects of the transaction, so he called the ServCorp CFO. The CFO offered Joe the flexibility to remain in active management or to exit, and assured Joe that ServCorp would offer to retain all or nearly all of MSC's employees, although a number would have to move to ServCorp's headquarters in Florida in order to retain their jobs. MSC's name would disappear. Joe realized that to make sure the offer really was the best available, he would have to hire a business broker to market his firm and solicit offers from other potential buyers.

Scenario 2: Management Buyout

Feeling uncomfortable with ServCorp's offer and wanting to avoid an auction for MSC, Joe asked the five MSC managers about the company and, after thinking about it and doing some reading, they said they were willing to take a risk and invest their own money in the company to buy Joe out. From Joe's perspective, the deal would be similar to one with an outside buyer, except the price would likely be lower and he would probably be financing more of the transaction. Let us say he would take $5 million for the company, $2 million in cash, and $3 million in the form of a seven-year note. He would pay 25% in long-term federal and state capital gains taxes over the term of the sale, plus tax on the interest on the note, leaving him with a net of $3.75 million on the value of the stock sold.

The managers would need to raise $400,000 each to find the cash for Joe. Where would it come from? They could use existing savings, borrow against their homes, or raise money from friends and family. Interest payments on the note to Joe might come out of their after-tax salaries (if they were currently receiving bonuses, the bonus money might also be now used for this purpose).

This raises two issues: First, the money used to buy Joe out would be after-tax; the managers already paid tax on it. So the $5 million would require roughly $8 million in pretax income. Second, some of the money would probably be borrowed, adding an additional debt payment to the purchase. Depending on the size and terms of the loan, that could add another several hundred thousand dollars to the cost. After accounting for taxes, this might (making some modest assumptions) add another $500,000 in costs, meaning those managers collectively would need pretax earnings of $8.5 million to buy the company.

Of course, added on to this is considerable risk. If the business did not generate enough income to provide the managers with the money needed to repay the debt, they could lose their homes. If the business failed, they would lose their investment as well.

But let us be more optimistic and assume the business would succeed. We'll also assume that each manager would own 20%. If the business value grew to $10 million 10 years later, a reasonable assumption for a modestly successful company, the managers would walk away with a $1.5 million profit ($10 million minus $8 million in pretax income needed to buy the business, minus the $500,000 in interest), or $300,000 each.

Scenario 3: ESOP

After he and the management team discussed the advantages and risks of the management buyout, they decided to investigate a sale to an ESOP for comparison. (For the sake of simplicity, this scenario assumes that the company would become 100% ESOP-owned and that the ESOP loan would be paid out over the course of 10 years. ESOPs do not need to own 100% of the shares, and an ESOP may stretch out the loan payment for longer than 10 years.)

One big difference is that the company, not the managers, would fund the ESOP's purchase by making contributions to the ESOP for it to repay its loan. Because an ESOP is a qualified employee benefit plan, that money would be tax-deductible. To become 100% ESOP-owned, the company might borrow some money from a lender and finance the rest with a note from Joe (but it could be 100% seller-financed or, less likely, 100% lender-financed as well). It would repay the loan through the ESOP in pretax dollars. So the $5 million purchase would cost $5 million, not $8 million.

The shares in the ESOP would be allocated to employee accounts based on their relative pay, counting pay up to $270,000 per employee (as of 2017). But all 50 employees would not be in the plan because some would not meet the typical ESOP requirement that employees work at least 1,000 hours in a plan year to be eligible for an allocation of shares from the ESOP. We'll assume here that 45 do. The 5 top managers would make much more than other employees, of course. Based on data we at the NCEO have gathered from ESOP companies, the top management generally would make about three to four times what the average worker would make. We'll assume here the 5 managers would have a total of $650,000 in "covered pay" (i.e., counting pay up to $270,000 per employee), while the 40 employees in the plan would have a total of $1.5 million (that is, they are about at the median wage). So of the $2.15 million in covered payroll, management would have about 30% and thus receive 30% of the allocations.

How much employees end up with in an ESOP also depends on vesting. In most cases, managers are more likely than other employees to remain employed long enough to reach full vesting. When an employee who is not fully vested leaves, his or her unvested shares are forfeited and reallocated to the remaining group. In this case, managers would get 30% of these forfeitures (allocated, as with company contributions, on the basis of relative pay) on top of the 30% of the existing ESOP-held shares they own through their portion of company contributions. A conservative estimate would be that since the forfeited shares largely come from nonmanagers (since they are more likely to leave), the managers' proportionate share of the ESOP will increase by about 10% over time, from 30% to about 33%.

So how does this work out in terms of financial value? Remember, managers would pay nothing for their ownership, so they would receive 33% of the company for no investment. Moreover, management's investment in the non-ESOP transaction investment would be in after-tax dollars. On the other hand, the debt the ESOP takes on might result in slower growth in stock value relative to the original $5 million purchase price (the management buyout would have no company debt). Data show that ESOP companies perform better post-ESOP than equivalent companies without one, partly because of employee motivation and partly because of tax benefits. In our case, for instance, the 100% ESOP would pay no income tax; the management buyout example company would. Still, one should be conservative and assume the value of the company after 10 years would not be as great as with the management buyout.

The management buyout example assumes the company would be worth $10 million after 10 years. The ESOP example assumes somewhat slower growth for the ESOP-owned company because of the debt, so that after 10 years the company would be worth $8 million (in fact, this is almost certainly far too conservative because ESOP companies tend to grow faster than non-ESOP companies and will overcome the debt issue in several years, but we're being cautious here). Management would own 33% of that, worth $2.64 million, or about $533,280 each. In the management buyout case, they would net $300,000. In other words, the ESOP turns out to be a better deal for management, even with management owning less of the company. Moreover, the managers could roll their ESOP distributions into an IRA on a tax-deferred basis.

In some ESOP companies, management may also get some additional equity in the form of stock appreciation rights or phantom stock. Where this is done, it might add another few percentage points to the ownership of each manager, making the deal even better.

Table 2-1 summarizes this comparison. The assumptions here are meant to be realistic and modestly conservative. But every example is very different in terms of how many managers are involved, how the management buyout is set up, payroll differences, turnover differences, and what happens to the company after the buyout. The point is not that managers or sellers are always better off with an ESOP approach, but rather that the kind of calculation shown here should be made before making a decision.

As the next section of this chapter explores in more depth, it is common for the ESOP to own only part of the company, leaving flexibility for managers to purchase additional stock and/or receive additional equity as incentives. So the five managers here might buy 30% of the

Table 2-1. Comparison of sale to outsiders, a management buyout, and an ESOP buyout

	Outside sale	Management buyout	ESOP buyout
Value of company at sale	$7 million	$5 million	$5 million
From the seller's perspective			
Take-home value to seller	$5.25 million	$4 million	$5 million
Form of payment	Combination of cash, stock, notes, other assets. Possible escrow or holdback.	Combination of cash, notes, other assets	Cash (and/or a note if seller-financed)
From the managers' perspective			
Company value 10 years later	Unknown	$10 million	$8 million*
Cost of purchase to managers	NA	$8.5 million ($8 million in pretax income, plus $500,000 in interest)	$0
Percentage owned by managers after 10 years	0%	100%	33%
Gain per manager, accounting for tax and interest costs	$0	$300,000	$533,280
Risk to managers if company fails	None	Any assets pledged against loans, such as homes	None
From the employees' perspective			
Benefits	Unknown	Likely unchanged	Larger **
Job security	Unknown	Likely unchanged	Slight improvement

* Reflects the effect of the debt the company must take on to make the purchase.

**ESOP participants have, on average, 2.5 times the retirement assets in company-sponsored plans relative to employees in comparable non-ESOP companies.

company, or they might acquire the rights to an additional 15% to 20% of the total equity value through stock appreciation rights, for instance, making the ESOP approach even more favorable to them.

Partial and Complete ESOP Sales

In the past, it was rare for an ESOP to buy 100% of a company all at once. Financing simply was not available because all forms of collateral are discounted to some degree and banks rarely wanted to make unsecured loans. With the advent of S corporation ESOPs and the rising popularity of seller financing, a transaction where 100% of the stock is sold to an ESOP has become much more common, either through seller notes alone or a combination of senior bank debt and subordinated seller notes.

Because the resulting entity pays no income tax (assuming the company is an S corporation), loan repayment is easier, making the loans less risky than might otherwise be the case. Nonetheless, any 100% transaction must be very carefully scrutinized. Making excessively optimistic projections about the ability to generate the necessary cash flow can easily lead a company into bankruptcy.

Though 100% sales are increasing, it is still more common for ESOPs to be done in stages. Either an existing owner wants to sell some stock now and some later or there is more than one owner and only one wants to sell. An ESOP is a particularly favorable way to do this because, unlike most buyers, it is perfectly content to buy a minority stake. There are, however, two caveats to keep in mind.

First, if the ESOP is buying a noncontrol interest, it pays a noncontrol price, meaning there is usually a discount of 25% or more (see the chapter on valuation in this book for more detail). Many, but not all, ESOP advisors believe that if there is a specific plan for the ESOP to buy control over a reasonable period of time, a control price can be paid in each transaction *provided* that the ESOP trustee is given governance control rights from the outset (but note the trustee is appointed by the board). If this is not what will happen, sellers have to be able to accept this discount. In some cases, especially where there are multiple owners, a seller might instead push for a complete sale of the company to maximize the share price.

Second, if there are multiple owners and debt is used to purchase shares, the debt will reduce the value of the shares held by owners who are not selling. That reduction goes away when the debt is repaid, but if they want to sell to the ESOP before that, they might get a lower price.

Myths

The NCEO's experience in talking with business owners, reporters, and policy makers is that they have preconceptions about ESOPs and even after doing research, they hold on to some myths. We discussed above some reasons that an ESOP might not make sense for a company, but the reasons below are simply invalid. If you are considering an ESOP, do not let these myths get in the way.

The employees don't have the funds to buy the company: That's true. They rarely do. But what is also true is that in an ESOP they do not use their own funds to buy the company. ESOPs are funded by corporate pretax contributions to the employee stock ownership trust. There can be annual discretionary cash contributions to buy shares each year, or the trust can borrow money to buy shares with the company making tax-deductible contributions to pay off the loan.

Companies have to make a fixed contribution every year: This is only true if an ESOP is used to repay a loan, not if the company is making annual discretionary contributions in cash to buy shares. Even with a loan, it may be possible to renegotiate a payment schedule.

Credit for an ESOP loan is not available: ESOP loans have a very low default rate (two per thousand), so banks that have some experience in this area typically will view them more favorably than other highly leveraged transactions. If bank credit is not available, however, sellers can finance the sale directly by taking a note with the ESOP paying an equivalent arms-length interest rate.

Management must share financial information with employees: There is no such rule. Companies need only provide annual account statements indicating the total value of the account, vesting, and stock value, plus other information relating to the ESOP itself, not corporate finances. The most effective ESOP companies are "open book," but it is their choice to do that.

ESOPs only work in certain kinds of companies: There are ESOPs in every industry, from fast-food restaurants to heavy industrial equipment manufacturers to architects and engineers to software companies. They are as small as 10 or so employees (we know one with 4) and as large as hundreds of thousands.

The employees will run the company: ESOPs are run by a trustee appointed by the board. In closely held companies, employees only must be able to direct the voting of their shares on a very limited number of issues, most notably sale of all or substantially all the assets of the company (but not on a stock sale), merger, or recapitalization. Employees do not have to be given the right to direct the voting of their shares for who is on the board, much less the right to determine who runs the company or how (albeit companies can choose to be more democratic).

Decision Factors

The sections above and the remainder of the book provide the information companies need to make an informed choice about whether to proceed with investigating an ESOP. To summarize some of the main points, here is a list of the main factors that drive the decision. Make sure you are not overlooking any of these in your decision-making process.

- Take-home value (the after-tax, after-expense value to the seller)
- Form of payment (cash, stock, notes, other assets)
- Terms (timing, contingencies, requirements, ongoing responsibilities)
- Partial sales
- Fate of the company and work force
- Projected profitability (both the amount of earnings and their stability)
- The ratio between enterprise value and payroll

- Impact of the sale on corporate culture
- The importance of the seller having a degree of post-transaction control
- The wishes and demands of other owners
- The risks of sale (market reaction, disclosures during due diligence, costs of failure)
- Strength of management team

Conclusion: Should You Sell to an ESOP?

There is no simple answer, and sellers need to do a careful financial assessment as well as determining whether the ESOP fits with their other personal goals. Making this decision is an important and time-consuming one. When it is made correctly with the right company, however, it can be both a financially and personally rewarding journey.

Thanks to Aaron Juckett of ESOP Partners for his thoughtful review of this chapter.

Chapter 3

Understanding ESOP Valuation

Corey Rosen

Why Do You Need a Valuation?

There is a T-shirt in the Exploratorium museum in San Francisco with a picture of Albert Einstein in a policeman's hat. The legend on the T-shirt says "186,000 miles per second. It's not just a good idea, it's the law." If you want to have an ESOP in a closely held company, an independent, outside valuation is not just a good idea, it's the law. You must have an appraiser figure out what a willing buyer would pay a willing seller, assuming both have all the relevant information they need to make the transaction. The law is designed to make sure the ESOP does not overpay for the shares when it buys shares for a non-participant shareholder and pays enough to participants selling back to the ESOP and the company.

Congress created this requirement because of a number of disturbing cases in which ESOPs paid considerably more than what an outside appraiser would have said was fair. But even absent this kind of abuse, it's still a good idea to get an independent valuation. If an owner is selling to an ESOP, a price determined by a formula or by the board, for instance, is almost certainly going to be wrong. Many people call us saying "Why can't we just use book value?" or some other formula. But book value usually understates the real worth of ownership in most businesses, just as most other formulas are misleading. Most businesses are worth some multiple of their earnings, earnings that are generated not just by assets, but by such intangibles as reputation, expertise, contacts, innovative ideas and processes, etc. On the other hand, a minority interest in a company may, in some cases, be worth less than a simple per-share book value calculation may suggest, and some businesses' assets may be worth more than the future earnings they can create in that particular enterprise (real estate may fit this definition, for instance). So if you are selling for book value, you are almost certainly not getting a correct price.

On the other hand, other owners call us and say they know that in their industry, businesses sell for an average of x times earnings or some other multiple. But your business is not likely to be average. If in using a formula you come up with a value that is just a few percentage points higher or lower than a more accurate assessment of your company's value, the costs will be much greater than the cost of a valuation. For instance, if your formula is off 3%, and your value is $2 million, then the formula is either costing you (if it is too low) or the ESOP (if it is too high) $60,000, many times the cost of an independent appraiser.

Second, an independent appraisal is essential to convincing employees that an ESOP is a good thing for them. If they believe that the ESOP is overpaying for its shares—that it is just a clever way, for instance, for the owner to take money out of the company on a tax-preferred basis—then employees are going to be very skeptical about the plan.

Third, an independent valuation can be critical if there are multiple owners. If one sells for too high or too low a price, an artificial benefit or cost is created for one party or the other. In many ESOPs, sales are done in stages. Too high a price in the first stage means the shares the seller continues to hold are worth less and the company may be put in unnecessary financial danger.

Finally, having an appraisal can be a useful business planning tool. After all, the appraiser's report, which typically runs 75 pages or so, is all about comparing your business both to other businesses and to other uses for the money invested in your company. It thus provides a detailed benchmark to determine how you are doing and what elements of your strategy can be changed to improve equity value.

How Often Must an Appraisal Be Performed?

The law requires appraisals to be done at least annually, but there may be circumstances that require a more frequent appraisal. The law also requires that ESOP transactions be conducted at the current fair market value. That means that any time the ESOP buys or sells stock, it should, in theory, be based on a fair market valuation as of the date of the transaction.

If the ESOP is buying shares from an owner or the company, for instance, it should try to time its purchase to coincide with the most recent appraisal as closely as possible. The IRS prefers that the transaction be accompanied by a valuation opinion letter stating that the valuation is effective as of that date. On an ongoing basis, in an ideal scenario all transactions related to plan distributions (such as a departing employee selling shares back to the company or the plan) occur at a specific annual date that is timed as closely as possible with the annual appraisal. In practice, what this usually means is that the appraiser provides a report on a regular schedule and the plan administrator closes the plan year as soon as possible after that. Statements are then mailed to employees, and transactions are completed during a short window following the closing.

But what happens if there is an ESOP transaction that is not in this window? Just how close is close enough? Unfortunately, there is no useful guidance on this. Say, for instance, that an appraisal is completed as of April 1 ("as of" here means that the price set in the report is effective that date, not that the report is completed that date). On July 1, the ESOP buys shares from an owner, or an employee sells stock back to the ESOP. Is the April 1 appraisal acceptable? The only answer is that the trustee of the ESOP—the person or persons who make decisions for the plan—must be able to show that there is no reason to believe that there will be any significant change in value over that time, either from internal factors (a change in the company's revenues, costs, assets, or other issues that affect value) or external factors (the market for equities has changed, such as a sharp drop in the S&P index or a hike in interest rates). Absent the ability to say that confidently, a new appraisal is needed. Your ESOP advisors should be looked to for guidance on these issues any time there is any doubt. For distributions to employees, plans can also state that distributions will occur as of the most recent appraisal, even though that could be up to one year old. If this is done consistently, it is normally acceptable unless there is reason to think there has been a very significant upward or downward movement in share price in the interim.

Who Hires the Appraiser?

The appraiser is hired by and reports to the trustee of the plan, not the seller or the board. Most trustees do not want the seller even to see the valuation report; some do not want board members to see it either, although on an ongoing basis, boards do normally get the valuation report or at least a detailed summary because it is so critical to understanding the business. While in practice the appraisal fees are normally paid for by the company, it is important that the contractual relationship be between the trustee and the appraiser. Thus, the recommendations directed to "you" below about hiring an appraiser are addressed to the ESOP trustee, and in particular an internal trustee (i.e., a company employee or committee) as opposed to an external trustee whose business it is to know these matters.

The fact that the appraiser's client is the ESOP trust, no matter who actually writes the checks to cover the fees, has important implications. First, the letter of engagement should clearly specify that the appraiser is working for the ESOP. Second, it means the appraiser is not trying to find the highest price that can be justified or, as in some tax-oriented appraisals, the lowest. Third, it should remind everyone involved that the point of the appraisal is to protect the interests of the ESOP participants by ensuring the ESOP does not pay more than fair market value in any purchase from an outside seller and that employees are paid fair market value for company shares in their ESOP accounts.

Who Performs an Appraisal?

The law requires an independent, outside appraisal from someone who is customarily in the business of doing business appraisals. There has never been a precise definition of what "independent" is, however. Clearly, some people are excluded—your board, your attorney, your brother-in-law, your CFO, your CPA, or anyone else with a direct financial relationship with the company. But what about your CPA firm (but not the person doing your books), or the valuation advisor who is affiliated with your attorney? Many people argue that if your CPA firm is large and can establish a "firewall" separating its audit and valuation sections, then that is acceptable. Others contend that even this is risky.

Similarly, some people say you can use firms affiliated with your advisers (such as a valuation firm that pays a fee to your attorney for referrals), but most experts would argue that is not a wise policy.

We strongly suggest that you pick a firm that has no other business relationship with your company than the appraisal itself. Almost all the lawsuits involving ESOPs concern valuation. The law looks primarily to process, not results, in determining whether the appraisal was fair to the ESOP. An appraisal done by a truly independent, qualified firm establishes a degree of credibility not possible any other way. With any other firm, there is always the possibility that the appraisal was done with an eye toward getting or keeping the company's business for the other parts of the firm or the affiliated parties involved in other parts of the transaction. The costs will rarely be lower in using someone not truly independent, so it is best to err on the side of caution.

A more difficult issue is whether a valuation firm that has done work for the firm before the ESOP should be hired by the trustee. The Department of Labor has been very focused on this issue in recent years, indicating it is very skeptical of appraisers who have any other relationship with the company. Appraisal firms that have done work unrelated to the ESOP should be excluded. A more difficult issue is whether an appraisal firm that is hired to do a preliminary appraisal for ESOP purposes can be used for the full-scale ESOP appraisal for the ESOP transaction. A preliminary appraisal can help a company decide whether to do an ESOP and to plan for financing it. Tim Hauser, a deputy assistant secretary at the Department of Labor, has argued that this is "road testing" the appraiser to see if a high enough price can be obtained, and says the DOL wants companies to use a different firm for the transaction than for the preliminary appraisal. Using a separate firm adds somewhat to cost, but it also means the preliminary appraisal may come to a somewhat different conclusion of value than would be obtained from the firm that will ultimately do the ESOP appraisal, albeit the difference is likely to be small. The most prudent approach is to use a different firm for the preliminary appraisal than for the transaction.

The other major issue in determining whether an appraiser is qualified is competence. Here there are two areas to evaluate. The first is general business appraisal competence. Anyone can be a business appraiser. No specific degree and no licensing procedure is required by states or other entities. The appraisal industry does try to be self-regulating, however.

There are a number of organizations, offering a wide variety of designations, that provide some kind of business appraisal certification. Among these are the American Society of Appraisers (ASA), the National Association of Certified Valuation Analysts (NACVA), the Institute of Business Appraisers (IBA), and the American Institute of Certified Public Accountants (AICPA). Each organization provides some kind of technical education program providing certification designations. There are so many designations now that they can become quite confusing. It is worth asking an appraiser what designations he or she has and what was required to obtain them, but making comparisons on designations alone may be difficult.

In addition to these qualifications, you should also look at experience, in-house training requirements for the firm, whether the appraiser has spoken or published on the subject, and, of course, references.

Business appraisal competence is not enough, however. As will become clear later, there are many ESOP-specific issues. These issues can have a dramatic impact on the final valuation. Your appraiser should be able to demonstrate specific experience and expertise in ESOPs. Ask for a list of ESOP clients and call them. Find out whether the appraiser belongs to the relevant professional organizations (the NCEO and the ESOP Association), regularly attends professional conferences on the subject, and has spoken or written on ESOP-specific issues. If the appraiser claims to have ESOP expertise but does not meet these criteria, look elsewhere.

How Do You Find a Good Appraiser?

Both the NCEO and the ESOP Association maintain lists of appraisers and other ESOP professionals that are available to members. Neither group endorses the people listed in the guides, but at least this provides assurance that the appraisers are involved in the relevant professional organizations. Most active ESOP appraisers will appear on both lists. Your other professional advisors usually will also have recommendations, and you should ask other ESOP companies whom they have used.

One issue to decide is whether to pick an appraiser from a large or small firm. Large firms typically have an appraisal reviewed by one or more other staff members and may have additional credibility should there be a legal challenge. Some small firms, however, have excellent reputations and also may provide for internal reviews. Generally, large firms charge more, but this is not always the case. While there is not a right or wrong answer here, size per se is probably not a critical issue when comparing firms of comparable price, competence, and compatibility.

In picking an appraiser, it is wise to interview at least two or three candidates. You will find that there are significant variations in price, experience, and appraisal philosophy. The first two are obvious things to look for, but the third may seem a little confusing. Why ask about philosophy?

Different ESOP appraisers have different approaches to key appraisal issues, such as discounts for lack of control or liquidity (these are discussed below), or in their general appraisal approach (such as whether they rely more on earnings multiples or on comparable companies). These will have a potentially dramatic effect on value. Initial assumptions tend to get locked into your ongoing ESOP appraisal. It will always arouse suspicion if, a few years after the first ESOP appraisal, you decide you are unhappy with the approach and choose someone else who comes in with a different set of assumptions. Your business won't have changed, but ESOP participants and the IRS may now see a very different appraisal number. At best, you have a serious communications problem; at worst, you have a lawsuit or problem with the government.

Similarly, it is both expensive and risky to decide after the initial appraisal that you do not like the result and ask to have a second appraisal from someone else. The appearance, at least, is that you are shopping for an appraisal advantageous to you, not accepting an objective report. To head off such complications, the ESOP trustee or the person who will become the trustee (as we shall see, the appraiser works for the trustee) should interview appraisers beforehand. If the ESOP trustee decides down the road that the appraisal is in some way potentially faulty, the best approach is to hire a third party to do a review of the appraisal report (but not redo the appraisal). This is fairly inexpensive. If the review is positive, then things can continue; if not, the trustee may seek some changes in approaches by the appraiser or decide to hire an alternative firm (but not the one doing the diagnostic).

Some appraisers, as well as some legal advisors, may tell you that this too makes it appear you are shopping the appraisal. But we at the NCEO would argue, along with most of the ESOP legal community, that without these discussions the trustee cannot make an informed decision on who is best to do the appraisal.

Now, however, comes the tricky part. These interviews must be designed to find out what approaches are going to be in the best long-term interest of the ESOP and its participants. The goal is not to find the appraiser who will come up with the highest price. Instead, the trustee should be looking to assure, as best as possible, that the appraisal will support the long-term viability of the plan and that the appraisal will use methodologies that are generally accepted by the appraisal community and the regulatory authorities. That means the price will not be so high as to endanger the company's ability to pay for it nor so low that the current sellers will not want to sell. The appraisal assumptions and procedures must also assure that future participant distributions will be at their proper value. The ultimate price must fit within the range of what reasonable appraisers could agree is not more than fair market value.

Admittedly, these are somewhat vague guidelines, but ESOP appraisal is an art, not a science. While the process cannot be exact, however, it can and must be informed. A careful discussion with the appraiser about these issues prior to engagement can avoid confusion and unhappiness down the line. Note, however, that the appraiser may (appropriately) say that an initial discussion does not provide enough information to make an assessment of which approaches will work best.

Is the Appraised Price the One the ESOP Pays?

Once the appraiser has provided a report saying what fair market value is, that is not the end of the story. Many people incorrectly assume that this is the price that the ESOP must pay. Instead, the law requires that the ESOP cannot pay *more* than this price when purchasing shares from a seller. Indeed, it is the responsibility of the ESOP trustee to negotiate the best price possible, which sometimes will be less than the appraised value.

This negotiation might take a number of tacks. In a few cases, the seller prefers to sell for a lower price, usually because of concerns about the ability of the ESOP to repay the loan or just because the owner wants to be generous. In others, the trustee argues that tax benefits to a seller to an ESOP should come partly back to the ESOP in the form of a lower price. It is the ESOP, after all, that justifies the lower price as a result of its tax advantages. In still other cases, the ESOP trustee is simply bargaining for a better deal and, given the lack of other options the seller may have, is able to exert some leverage.

These scenarios all envision using an ESOP to buy shares from an existing owner. Sometimes an ESOP acquires new shares, such as when it borrows money to purchase shares to help finance growth, or when it accepts contributions of shares. In these cases, the trustee has less negotiating leverage because the contributions to the ESOP are diluting other owners, not buying their shares. Still, the size of a loan might be such that a lower price is needed to fit within legal requirements, or owners may wish to add another bargain element for the ESOP.

What Does the Appraiser Need from You?

In preparing an appraisal report, the appraiser will need a lot of data from you. The more precise and well prepared these data are, the better (and possibly cheaper) the appraisal will be. The following list indicates the key items appraisers generally need, although there may be other things requested:

- Financial statements, typically for the last five to ten years, preferably audited (but many smaller companies will present only reviewed statements). Income statements, balance sheets, cash flow and capital statements, and any explanatory footnotes or other material are included.
- Budgets or projections
- List of subsidiaries, if any
- Leases and contracts
- Compensation schedules
- Prior appraisals
- Dividend history and expectations

- Legal documents

- Prior sales or offers

- Shareholder list

- ESOP documents

- Operational information, such as sales by customer, patents, departmental budgets, competitors, etc.

In addition to a review of these documents, the appraiser will want to interview management and possibly board members, suppliers, customers, advisors, or anyone else deemed to have critical information. One or more site visits will be arranged. During these interviews, any significant issues that could materially affect operations, such as a pending environmental liability, a new competitor, management changes, or a patent expiration, for instance, should be thoroughly discussed.

What Is in the Appraisal Report?

Valuation reports typically run from 30 to 90 pages. The report will cover several issues. The basis for the appraisal of the company as an enterprise should be thoroughly explained and justified (for instance, if the appraiser chose to use an earnings ratio as a key element, why that was more appropriate in this case than some other methodology). Then there should be a discussion of any discounts or premiums applied to that value for the shares the ESOP is purchasing. Again, a thorough explanation of assumptions and rationale should appear. The data used for making the determination should be outlined, and any weightings or judgments used in assessing these data should be elaborated. Any special factors that affect valuation findings, such as a change in management that could reduce future value, should be covered. Reports usually also include a number of charts and tables showing different indications of value based on different methods.

In addition to these matters, the report should follow the guidelines included in the Department of Labor's proposed regulations concerning valuation. Among other things, these include a discussion of the business, its markets, and general economic considerations affecting value. The company's book value should be considered, along with any goodwill or other intangible assets and the company's dividend-paying history and capacity. The price of similar companies, if any, should be provided. Finally, issues relating to marketability and control concerns need to be reviewed. The trustee needs to show that the process for selecting an appraiser has been thorough and resulted in the selection of a legitimate ESOP valuation expert. The trustee must also show that the financials provided to the appraiser are accurate and realistic, not best-case scenarios. In ongoing valuations, the appraiser should be able to demonstrate how the repurchase obligation has been factored into the final price.

The final valuation will be a blending of these issues. Because there is no formula for valuations, however, each report will be different.

Steps in the Valuation Process: What Is Fair Market Value and How Is It Calculated?

In calculating how much the ESOP can pay, the first step is to determine how much the business is worth as an entity. There are three basic approaches used to determine this: the asset approach, the market approach, and the income approach.

Asset Approach

This is the simplest approach and one many closely held companies already use to value their shares for purchases by key employees. It is also the least used method in ESOP appraisals. In this approach, a company is assessed based on either the liquidation value of its assets or its adjusted book value. The adjusted net asset methodology approach takes the balance sheet and transforms it from an accounting document to an economic one. For instance, an asset may be fully depreciated on the balance sheet, but still have resale value on the market. Liabilities may not appear on the balance sheet because they are contingent, such as a possible environmental issue (cleaning up a landfill, for instance). Inventories also need to be adjusted for what they could currently sell for in the market. Any accounts receivable and payable not on the balance sheet need to be considered. Any intangible, but marketable, assets (such as a trade name) need to be assessed.

While these methods are simple, they are also usually wrong. People usually want to buy a business because it can yield them a return on their investment; the ESOP always looks at a purchase this way. While a company's assets are part of what creates an income stream in a company, they are only part of it. All sorts of other factors—expertise, reputation, contacts, processes, labor practices, and other issues—condition how much a company can make. The asset approach has even less relevance when only a minority stake is being sold because minority owners cannot force a liquidation of assets.

Market Approach

The next approach is to see what, if any, evidence there is of how much people would pay for stock in the company or comparable companies. There may be, for instance, a history of stock sales in the company, or there could be other valid offers. These offers, however, do not necessarily establish a value that the ESOP can pay.

First, the offers may have been for control when the ESOP is not buying control (or vice-versa). Stock is worth more when it is part of a control purchase, as discussed more fully below. Second, the offer may have come from another company with a synergistic interest in the target company. If International MegaCompany can gain operating efficiencies, or eliminate competition, by buying Pete's Pizza Parlors, they will pay more for Pete's than would a buyer who could not capture these efficiencies. The ESOP is always a *financial* buyer; it must be able to justify its purchase based on the return that investment yields as a stand-alone company, although heavy acquisition activity in a given industry may influence market pricing upward and should be considered. Third, the offer or sale may have been for less than market value, as often is the case with sales to managers based on book value. These and similar concerns make this methodology useful in providing benchmarks, but far from determinative.

A related methodology is to look at comparable companies. The ideal comparison is another closely held company in the same industry with similar financials. But these ideal companies are hard to find, and, even if found, there are usually only limited data on transactions, not the detailed information to allow apples-to-apples comparisons (such as whether the sale was to a synergistic buyer). Private companies do not have to report such data to any public source, but some valuation companies have access to databases that track sales that their firm has followed.

Better data are available from public companies, but here several complicating issues arise. First, many public companies have multiple lines of business. Second, they are almost always larger, and often much larger, than the company being appraised. Third, they may have very different capital structures than closely held companies. These and other differences make direct comparisons difficult. Most business appraisers are experienced in dealing with these complications, however, so the data on stock prices in these companies can yield useful insights about the typical ratios (such as share price to annual earnings) that can be applied, with appropriate adjustments, to provide benchmarks for applying multiples to the company being valued. When using public companies, the indicated value for the company being appraised is a minority interest, freely marketable value because the share prices of the publicly traded companies represent small minority interests in the public company.

Another source of market data is comparable companies (including closely held companies) that have been merged and/or acquired. Multiples paid in such comparable transactions are generally applied, with appropriate adjustments, to the subject company's earnings and cash flow. Because the multiples based on these data are calculated using prices paid for entire companies, the indicated value for the subject company is a value for the entire company (enterprise or control value). It may or may not indicate a "liquid" value, depending on whether or not the comparable merged and/or acquired companies were public or privately held at the time of acquisition.

However a market approach is constructed, a company's earnings will be "normalized" to reflect how another buyer would operate the business. This is discussed in more detail below in the section on the income approach to valuation.

Income Approach

A third set of methodologies falls under the income approach. The basic theory behind these methodologies is that a buyer is looking to make a reasonable return on an investment over an acceptable period of time, given the relative risk of the investment. A theoretical willing buyer is looking at a variety of investment choices. There are safe ones with low returns (CDs, T-bills, etc.), somewhat riskier ones with higher returns (stocks and bonds), and still riskier ones with the highest returns (individual companies). It has to be this way: the higher the risk, the greater the return an investor will demand. In buying a company, then, the investor needs to know two basic things: what the risk is and what the income flow is that will result from the investment. There are a number of ways to conceptualize these factors, but the two most common are referred to as capitalization of free cash flow and discounted cash flow.

Capitalization of free cash flow method: With the capitalization of free cash flow (FCF) method, the appraiser develops an estimate of the company's sustainable level of free cash flow. This is usually based on history and estimates of what future FCF will be. FCF is defined as follows:

> Net income
> + Non-cash charges (such as depreciation)
> − Increases in working capital
> + Additions to long-term debt
> − Payments of long-term debt
> − Capital expenditures
> = Free cash flow (FCF)

Free cash flow is normally used because that is the basis from which an investor can earn a return from the investment either in the form of dividends or investment of the FCF back into the business for future growth. However, some appraisers prefer other variations on the future income theme, such as earnings before interest, taxes, and depreciation.

After these numbers are determined, they are adjusted to reflect nonrecurring items and special considerations. For instance, there may have been a large one-time expense that lowered earnings (and thus FCF) in a prior year, or an anticipated one-time expense in the future projections. Very commonly the pay and perquisites of executives or other employees needs to be adjusted to reflect what the market rates for these individuals are, unless these practices will remain in place after the transaction. If the CEO is making $700,000 a year and has a company-paid vacation to France every year, the appraiser might determine that these expenses would be substantially reduced if someone else bought the company. This excess is added back to earnings if the levels of compensation will not continue into the future. Similar adjustments to earnings and cash flow are typically made before applying multiples in the market approaches as well. After analyzing historical and potential earnings, the appraiser will determine a single figure called "representative earnings."

Finally, a capitalization rate is applied to these representative cash flows. The concept here involves some complex math, but the basic idea is simple. The appraiser is trying to determine what the present value of a future stream of sustainable FCF is. The rate is derived by subtracting the expected long-run rate of FCF growth from the company's discount rate. The discount rate, in turn, reflects the rate of available risk-free investments and the risk adjustments appropriate for the fact that this is an equity investment made in a company of a certain size (there is less risk in a large company) with specific risk concerns.

For instance, an appraiser might determine that in a particular business, the expected FCF growth rate is 6% per year. The discount rate is 25%. The capitalization rate is now 19%, and this is divided into expected FCF to determine the company's value. If the next year's (or sustainable) FCF is $3 million, the company would be worth $3 million divided by .19, or $15.8 million before considering appropriate discounts or premiums. The underlying concept here is that the investor is looking to obtain a return on investment that justifies the risk. In this case, the return would be 19% on the expected annual FCF.

Discounted cash flow approach: A similar approach is the discounted cash flow method. Here the discount rate (25% in this case) is applied to a measure of FCF. Theoretically, all the earnings could be paid out this way to justify the investment, and this would provide a benchmark for determining value. Again, annualized free cash flows are determined; these are then discounted back to the present at the required rate of return or discount rate. The appraiser will add a terminal value at the end of the forecast period to complete the analysis.

In both methods, attention must be paid to the special tax benefits the ESOP provides the company as these can change expected earnings and cash flow. The discount rates used above are for simple math purposes. The rates vary over time and with a variety of factors, such as interest rates. In recent years, discount rates of 15% to 19% have been common.

What Discounts or Premiums Apply to ESOP Value?

Whether or not any discounts and/or premiums apply to the indicated values derived using the valuation methods described above depends on numerous factors. In ESOP valuations, discounts generally fall into two categories: liquidity and control. These are discussed in more detail below. But before knowing whether to apply a discount, it first must be determined whether or not the valuation is being conducted on a controlling interest (or enterprise) basis or a minority interest basis. Then, depending on the method and data used within the valuation method, appropriate discounts and/or premiums are applied. Similarly, whether to apply a liquidity discount depends on whether the comparisons used to determine value are based on liquid or illiquid interests in companies.

By way of example, assume that the valuation assignment is to determine the enterprise (controlling interest) value of a company and that the appraiser has used market approaches and an income approach. In the market approach, the appraiser used two subsets of information, comparable publicly traded companies and comparable companies that had been merged and/or acquired.

As noted earlier, the value indicated based on comparable publicly traded companies is a minority interest, freely traded (or completely liquid) value. Therefore, in order to arrive at a value for an entire enterprise, it would generally be appropriate to apply a premium for control and a discount for lack of marketability. Conversely, if the valuation assignment were to value the company on a minority interest basis, it would not be appropriate to apply a minority interest discount to the comparable publicly traded approach, because the value indicated already reflects a minority interest discount. It would, however, be appropriate to consider a discount for lack of marketability.

The value indicated from the comparable merged and/or acquired company approach represents an indication of control or enterprise value. Thus, if the subject company is being appraised on a controlling interest basis, then it is not appropriate to apply a control premium to this approach. That would be a double discount because the value is already reflective of controlling interest value since the multiples used in this approach are based on prices paid for entire companies. On the other hand, if the subject company is being valued on a minority interest basis, then it would be appropriate to apply a minority interest discount to this approach. Whether or not a discount for lack of marketability is appropriate using this approach generally depends on if the comparable merged or acquired companies were public at the time of the acquisitions.

The income approach may indicate either a control or minority interest value. Generally speaking, if control level free cash flows were used, the income approach indicates a control value. If minority interest level free cash flows were used, the income approach generally indicates a minority interest value. However, variations in the discount rate and/or free cash flows used may result in some sort of blended indication of value, the subject of which is beyond the scope of this chapter.

The critical element to understand with regard to whether or not discounts and/or premiums are appropriate is that it *depends on the base from which the premiums and/or discounts are proposed.* If discounts are needed, they generally fall into two categories below: liquidity and control.

Liquidity and Repurchase Obligation Issues

If you buy shares in IBM, you can sell them any time and get your money in three days. If you buy stock in Sally's Computers, there is no ready market for the shares. You might not be able to sell them for years, and you may have to settle for less than market price if you need the money and no one is eager to buy. This lack of marketability creates a discount over the price for the sale of otherwise comparable shares in a public company or shares in a closely held company about to be sold (because in this case there is immediate liquidity). So in any closely held company selling shares other than in a total sale, there is a discount over what the price would be for publicly traded shares, usually in the range of 20% to 40% depending on the circumstances, such as any restrictions on the sale of stock, buy-sell agreements, prospects of an initial public offering, dividends, or the availability of other buyers.

Many ESOP appraisers contend that the presence of the ESOP mitigates or even eliminates this discount. ESOP rules require that departing employees have the right to put their shares back to the company (or have the company fund the ESOP to do this) at fair market value. This seems to eliminate the lack of marketability.

The reality is more complicated, however. First, there must be some assurance that the company can really muster the cash to repurchase the shares. Second, the put option does not belong to the ESOP, for which the appraisal is being made, but the participants in the plan. Third, the put option applies only in a limited window of time and only when people leave the company or can diversify their accounts. That is hardly the equivalent to owning shares in a public company.

Appraisers argue back and forth on the legal and practical issues involved here. The typical discount for lack of marketability in an ESOP company, according to NCEO studies, is 5% to 15%. A higher discount may discourage the seller from selling; one that is too low saddles the ESOP with an obligation on an ongoing basis to buy shares at a price that reflects an aggressive assumption about value (because these assumptions normally have to be carried forward).

In some appraisals, the liquidity discount is where the repurchase obligation is reflected. In that case, setting a liquidity discount should not simply consist of picking some round number that seems reasonable. The obligation of a company sponsoring an ESOP to buy back shares from departed ESOP participants represents a future use of nonproductive assets. This obligation means money is not available for other uses. If the company "recycles" the shares, either by contributing cash to the ESOP to buy the stock or by buying the stock directly and recontributing it to the ESOP immediately or over time, then the number of outstanding shares remains the same, while the discounted future cash flow per share declines by the magnitude of the obligation. This should produce an iterative set of calculations. The obligation will lower value, but the new lower value means a lower future obligation. The calculations keep being repeated until a solution is found. The resulting number should be a precise one, just as other elements of the valuation are, not just a "best guess."

On the other hand, if the company redeems shares and does not recontribute them, then the number of shares drops proportionately to the decreased future cash flow, producing a neutral effect on share value but reducing enterprise value.

An emerging (and we think better) practice for the repurchase obligation, however, is to calculate the amount of the obligation over the coming years that is in excess of what the company would normally pay for benefits. This results in lower projected earnings. That results in a lower value, which makes the repurchase smaller, so the calculation is run again (and again and again in what is called an iterative process) until a solution is found. This calculation is affected by how much cash is in the ESOP, recycling versus redemption policies, and other factors.

Including the repurchase obligation in the valuation requires the appraiser to have a copy of a repurchase analysis. Companies that do not go through this process, and do not require the appraiser to factor it into the final result, will overpay for the shares, endangering the future ability of the company to grow or to honor its repurchase obligation.

Lack of Control (Minority Interest) Discounts and Control Premiums

The second major issue is control. When someone buys a controlling interest in a company, a premium is paid. This is why share values soar in takeover battles. If the ESOP is buying less than control, it pays less per share (a "minority interest") than would a buyer of controlling interest. Studies of control premiums in public company transactions are compiled every year. These typically are in the 30% range, but can vary widely. Again, however, note that it is only appropriate to apply a minority interest discount to a value indication that represents control.

The first source of variation in control premiums is the company's specific situation. In some companies, a 33% stake may carry some limited control rights; in others, even a 51% stake may not convey full control rights. There might be specific shareholder agreements that limit control of any owner, such as a buy-sell agreement, covenants with banks, or contractual obligations. These and other issues make control a more complex concept than "control" or "no control"; there are shadings in between as well.

A second source of variation is what the ESOP will buy in the future. If the ESOP starts at a minority stake but has a right to buy enough to get control in the future, can it pay a control price? Is the seller obliged to sell to the ESOP? Many advisors say yes, provided that the option allows the purchase in not more than three to five years and gives the ESOP trustee control rights even before gaining a numerical controlling interest. Some appraisers take a tougher view, some a more liberal one. Some appraisers even argue that if the ESOP is buying less than 51% in any purchase, it pays a non-control price (for instance, if the ESOP owns 51% and buys another 20%, it would pay a non-control price for this 20%). There are no right or wrong answers, although in all things related to valuation, we would urge a cautious approach.

Note, however, that the decision on whether to pay a control price is not one the appraiser makes. It is the trustee's decision. The appraiser can provide advice on this issue, but the trustee must decide whether the ESOP really has the attributes and rights necessary to allow a control price to be paid.

The Impact of Leverage on Valuation

If the ESOP borrows money, it will have an impact on valuation. The interest expense on the new debt the company now has taken on to fund the ESOP will show up on the balance sheet and, in any event, represents a significant non-productive expense. While this generally will not reduce value dollar-for-dollar (there are ESOP tax benefits, the company may grow, and there is a discount for the future value of money), it will reduce the post-transaction value. This effect will disappear as the loan is repaid.

This impact is important for two reasons. First, employees need to understand why this drop occurs. Their own account values start at the lower value and thus are not reduced by the debt (unless the loan is to a previously existing plan), but they need to understand the issue to avoid communications problems. Other owners will also see their share price drop, of course. If they plan to sell before the ESOP loan is repaid, this could present a problem. In some cases, companies arrange for pro-rata sales from owners to avoid this issue.

Advanced Issues

Valuation is obviously a complex subject. This chapter is only a basic introduction and cannot go into some of the more advanced scenarios that come up in ESOP appraisals. Two, however, deserve brief attention.

One is where an S corporation sets up an ESOP. When the ESOP trustee receives a statement of the pro-rata share of earnings on which taxes would be paid each year, the trustee can ignore it. ESOPs do not have to pay tax on their share of the S corporation's earnings. Clearly, S status with an ESOP can enhance earnings, yet, just as clearly, a potential willing buyer would be unlikely to maintain the ESOP. So from that buyer's standpoint, the future earnings would be unaffected by this special tax benefit. As a result, the standard practice in ESOPs is now to not "tax effect" the earnings. However, over time, the tax savings will help the company grow faster and more profitably.

A second issue occurs when there are multiple investors in a transaction with the ESOP. For instance, if the ESOP buys 30% of a company with debt to be paid out of future corporate earnings, while other investors put in hard cash to buy the remaining 70%, should both parties get a dollar-for-dollar allocation? The Department of Labor seems to think so, but ESOP appraisers have developed techniques for using stock with different attributes to allocate equity in a more realistic manner. If your company is this situation, it is vital to review allocation policy closely with advisors.

Conclusion

The requirement to have an ESOP appraisal is designed to assure that the ESOP process is fair to all parties involved. While many business owners would prefer to set their own prices using a formula or a number derived from prior offers, these simplistic approaches rarely result in the price the ESOP would pay as a financial buyer. ESOP trustees, as well as owners, managers, and employees of ESOP companies, need to understand the valuation process well.

Chapter 4

Financing the Leveraged ESOP

Kenneth E. Serwinski

Borrowing money to finance a leveraged employee stock ownership plan (ESOP) can be a challenge for closely held companies. Most successful business owners have learned that debt management over a long period of time can be quite demanding. Financing a leveraged ESOP actually recapitalizes the company, which is necessary to fund this exit strategy for existing shareholders. The bottom line is that the business owners are replacing equity with nonproductive debt. The strategy behind structuring a good transaction is to minimize the effects on the balance sheet and cash flows so ongoing working capital and capital expenditure needs are not inhibited. There is an overriding assumption in this process that the financial information available is good information. Before considering structuring issues, one should understand some of the credit criteria necessary to obtain this type of loan.

The Four C's of Lending

When deciding whether to grant a loan, lenders often base their decision on what are commonly known as the four C's of lending: character, cash flow, collateral, and capital.

Character

In evaluating an ESOP's feasibility in a closely held business, an honest assessment of the existing management is necessary. The success of an ESOP will be determined by management's ability to create a culture that will allow the new ESOP company to thrive. Inexperienced management could hinder the establishment of a successful ESOP.

When reviewing a phased ESOP transaction, one must consider the expected future involvement of the current business owner. In a phased ESOP transaction, the owner remains involved while creating an employee ownership environment and discovering new managerial talent. Many companies establish an ESOP to give quality management personnel the opportunity to demonstrate themselves as the owner's true successor. As a control transaction occurs, the lender places greater emphasis on the depth of management than on the involvement of the former owner. In the case of a 100% transaction, there is a mandate for a high level of confidence that the successor management is sound.

Finally, lenders look to the credit history of both the owner and the company to understand the true character of each. A poor credit payment history, combined with litigation problems, would certainly turn off most lenders.

Cash Flow

Most successful ESOPs result from successful companies. To analyze the effects of an ESOP loan on the company, advisors tend to look for good historical trends of profitability and cash flow. More importantly, one should study realistic projections of the company and its profitability during the course of the loan's amortization period. Projections can be difficult to rely upon; however, most companies can project the next two years' performance with some reliability. Because the ESOP loan, which represents nonproductive debt, is being put in place, the debt service coverage that most lenders look for would be in the range of 1.25 to 1.75 times cash flow. This is an indicative range. Some aggressive lenders may agree to a lower multiple for the first two years of the loan and establish a provision for a larger cushion over time.

Last but not least, because this is nonproductive debt, the company needs to satisfy its ongoing working capital and capital expenditure requirements. Thus, the company must have access to further credit if it cannot finance growth internally. The key is to structure a deal that will allow the company to continue to grow despite the addition of ESOP debt. The combination of understanding historical trends and future projections, along with adequate debt service coverage and access to additional credit, are important factors in structuring an ESOP loan that will not "kill" the company.

Collateral

The company generally must make collateral available for any loan it makes, including an ESOP loan. The lender, which always requires a second "way out" of a loan, will liquidate this collateral if chronic cash flow shortfalls occur. Once the collateral is known, its strength must be determined. Most businesses in a manufacturing environment have accounts receivable, inventory, equipment, and real estate available as collateral. Some of those assets, however, may already be used as collateral for the working capital, lines of credit, equipment loans, or real estate mortgages. If, however, some of the longer-term assets, such as equipment and real estate, are unencumbered, such assets might make reasonable forms of collateral to many lenders. Ideally, long-term loans should always be collateralized with these fixed assets.

If, as in the case of service businesses, there are limited fixed assets available for collateral, other alternatives may need to be considered. The most prominent alternative in service businesses is the pledging of Section 1042 replacement securities. (Section 1042 of the Internal Revenue Code allows the owner of a closely held C corporation to defer taxation of gains on stock he or she sells to an ESOP if the ESOP owns 30% of the company's stock after the sale and the selling shareholder reinvests, or "rolls over," the proceeds in qualifying replacement securities.)

Capital

After addressing whether the company has enough management infrastructure to make an ESOP loan work, whether the company has enough cash flow to handle the debt, and whether the lender feels comfortable with the collateral available, the next task is to understand the company's capital base. Adding an ESOP term loan will significantly affect the company's balance sheet and leverage, as tables 4-1 and 4-2 below illustrate. Table 4-1 demonstrates that the company has total liabilities of $8 million against a net worth of $6 million, producing a leverage ratio of 1.33 to 1.

After the $3 million ESOP loan is implemented, the total liabilities increase to $11 million, and there is a contra hit to equity of a similar dollar amount increasing the leverage from 1.33 to 1 to 3.67 to 1 (table 4-2).

Table 4-1. Balance sheet before stock purchase ($3,000,000 loan to buy 33% of outstanding shares)

Current assets	$8,000,000	Current liabilities	$5,000,000
Fixed assets	6,000,000	Long-term liabilities	3,000,000
Total assets	$14,000,000	Total liabilities	$8,000,000
		Net worth (assets – liabilities)	$6,000,000
		Leveraged ratio	1.33 to 1

Table 4-2. Balance sheet after stock purchase ($3,000,000 loan to buy 33% of outstanding shares)

Current assets	$8,000,000	Current liabilities	$5,000,000
Fixed assets	6,000,000	ESOP loan	3,000,000
Total assets	$14,000,000	Long-term liabilities	3,000,000
		Total liabilities	$11,000,000
		Net worth (assets – liabilities)	$3,000,000
		Leveraged ratio	3.67 to 1

ESOP Loan Structure

From the previous discussion, one can understand that structuring an ESOP loan can be quite challenging. Not only is the impact of the ESOP loan an issue; one must also be concerned with future working capital and capital expenditure needs so as not to encumber the company in such a manner that future growth is prohibited. ESOP loans are usually structured as follows:

Loan. A loan can be made either to the company or to the ESOP trust. Most lenders prefer to make ESOP loans to the company, since the loan then becomes a direct obligation of the company. The company in turn will make a loan at substantially the same terms and conditions to the ESOP trust. The internal loan amortization will most likely be different from an external loan and dictate share allocation and employee retirement benefits. A minority of lenders would consider loaning directly to the ESOP trust, but only if the company guaranteed the loan.

Amortization. ESOP loans typically have amortization periods of from five to ten years, with five- to seven-year full payout terms being the most popular. Most lenders are quite reluctant to go longer than ten years, and even then there will probably be a balloon payment after year five and certainly after year seven.

Collateral. Lenders may ask for collateral that ranges from Section 1042 replacement securities to receivables, inventory, equipment, and real estate.

Covenants. The imposition of covenants is directly related to the level of debt inside the company. It is not unusual, however, for lenders to have covenants for minimum cash flow coverage or debt service along with covenants for net worth to be kept at certain levels. Additionally, restrictions may be placed on seller note principal payments, dividend payments, amounts of capital expenditures, and bonus and compensation limits for existing shareholders.

Guarantees. Selling shareholders often must give personal guarantees, which can be a sticking point for them. The quality of collateral and the level of cash flow may determine whether and to what degree personal guarantees are necessary. Some guarantees cover collateral shortfalls. For example, if a borrower seeks a $2 million ESOP loan and the bank, understanding the liquidation value of the assets being pledged, finds that the borrower is a half million dollars short in collateral, the bank will require a limited guarantee only up to that half million dollars. When Section 1042 rollover securities are pledged, the quality of the collateral is such that some lenders will forgo the personal guarantee to obtain 100% liquid collateral. Interestingly, in the case of 100% transactions (or movement to 100%), personal guarantees are not required. Though this seems counterintuitive, this is because the company has been sold in its entirety. Sellers are not asked for guarantees because there is no consideration for them to do so.

What the Lender Will Ask For

Ideally, the lender, in considering the proposal for an ESOP loan, will look for at least three to five years of historical financial information. Financial statements must, at a minimum, be reviewed; preferably, they should be audited. In addition to financial statements, the lender will look for pro forma projections for both the income statement and the balance sheet. Providing the projections is just the beginning. Notes to those projections should include the assumptions underlying them. For example, where improvements in operating margins that have not occurred in the past are projected into the future, the reason for the improvement must be revealed. These pro forma projections must also include potential cost reductions, which can occur in many ways. Perhaps the selling shareholder is willing to reduce his or her salary to enhance the cash flow position. Alternatively, the company and its employees may decide to freeze or cut back wages to make the ESOP work.

Finally, the lender will ask for a report on available collateral. This will include an accounts receivable aging; an inventory breakdown, if appropriate, between raw materials, work in process and finished goods inventory; a fixed assets schedule; and appraisals of fixed assets as well as of the availability of the Section 1042 rollover securities as collateral.

The Borrower's Perspective

Although we have been reviewing what a lender might consider important in making an ESOP loan, it is appropriate to consider the borrower's perspective as well. ESOP financing has significant advantages over traditional forms of debt. The owner has probably looked at other exit strategies and determined that they are not appropriate for his or her particular company. There are few exit strategies available to the business owner, namely:

- *An initial public offering.* Taking the company public is not a complete exit strategy for the business owner. It can, however, be a phased exit strategy for the right kind of business.

- *Selling the business outright.* Selling the business to a third party is a definite consideration for many business owners. However, most buyers of a business do not pay completely in cash. They may pay a significant portion of the price, somewhere between 40% to 70%, as a down payment, but some form of seller financing may be required. Thus, the business owner becomes a partner with a buyer he or she does not really know.

- *Recapitalization for a family or management buyout.* To fund a family or management buyout, a significant amount of debt, either senior debt or senior/subordinated debt, may be required to effect a transfer of ownership. This can incur significant levels of debt, with the amortization of the loans being made with after-tax dollars.

- *Recapitalization using an ESOP.* This is a tax-advantaged form of recapitalizing the business for shareholders to realize value and liquidity. Because the ESOP is a qualified retirement plan, the company can make contributions to the ESOP on a pretax basis. This feature allows for amortizing the ESOP loan, both principal and interest, on a tax-deductible basis.

What Should the Borrowers Look For?

Borrowers must find lenders experienced in ESOP financing. Lenders and their counsel who are inexperienced with ESOPs need a tremendous amount of "handholding" to effect the transaction. When evaluating proposals from lenders, terms and conditions play a significant role. Look for favorable terms in amortization schedules, collateral, and guarantees. Rates and fees are certainly important, but realize that the lender is actually being asked to finance a leveraged buyout of existing shareholders and that rates and fees may reflect that level of risk. Be sure to take an active role in the selection of bank counsel that will document the financing transaction. If legal counsel is not familiar with the various nuances of ESOP financing, do not allow the bank to engage their services. Demand experienced counsel; doing so will significantly control your legal costs.

Alternative Financing Strategies

As a general rule, owners of closely held businesses shy away from leveraging up the balance sheet of their company. Thus, the idea of a leveraged ESOP scares them. There may be other alternatives that still allow owners to consider a leveraged ESOP. Some companies have significant amounts of corporate cash or marketable securities. Such a company can self-finance a leveraged ESOP. Companies with this type of cash and investments on hand, however, are rare.

With business owners wary of capital markets, a significant number of ESOPs have used seller financing to either partially or fully fund the transaction. Seller notes can take much less time to set up than bank loans and can be less costly because the bank often requires additional and sometimes costly additional paperwork (and legal fees that may go with it). Because banks often ask sellers to pledge personal assets for the note anyway, many sellers see seller notes as carrying no greater risk.

In a typical seller-financed transaction, the seller takes a note from the company (which then reloans it to the ESOP, much as in a bank loan structure) at a stated rate of interest that reflects not more than what an equivalent arms-length loan would pay given the risk. Interest rates range from a low of the minimum applicable federal rate (AFR) published by the Internal Revenue Service up to a rate of 8%, with the majority falling in the 4%–6% range. The terms of the two loans do not have to match. For a variety of reasons, it is preferable for the seller note not to be made directly to the ESOP, most notably that there is a lot more flexibility in the case of default and how rapidly shares get released from the ESOP suspense account. A 2011 NCEO survey indicated the notes were typically in the 5% to 8% range, but will vary with market conditions. The company issues a note to the ESOP and makes contributions to the trust to repay it. The seller note will be subordinated to any senior lender. Seller-financed notes can be "refinanced" with a third-party lender at any time during the payback period should the company decide it is prudent.

In some cases (perhaps as many as 20%, according to the NCEO survey), the seller notes have a more complex structure. Seller notes can be structured with 10- to 20-year amortization schedules and a balloon payment, for example. Interest rates can reflect competitive market rates, and the yield on the notes can be enhanced with a warrant feature. (In this context, a warrant is essentially a right to purchase a fixed number of securities at the value they have at the sale to the ESOP for some number of years into the future.)

The warrant is a financial instrument that gives the warrant holder the right, but not the obligation, to participate in the performance of the underlying security. When the warrants are issued, a strike price is set. The strike price may be the underlying stock price at the time of the transaction. These traditional warrants act as a kind of sweetener that allows the issuer (company) to offer a lower coupon rate. Over time, the warrants build value as the stock price increases (i.e. current stock price - the strike price = warrant value). The value of the warrants will be paid to the holder on the expiration date.

A seller would receive a coupon rate of interest on the note with the warrant, providing a market rate of return reflective of a note subordinated to a lender or bonding company. Hence, the mechanics for the seller are to take part of his or her payment on the note in the form of interest and part in a warrant, in effect receiving current return in interest and future consideration in warrants for x number of shares at the time of the sale and receiving the right to buy those additional shares at that price for some number of years into the future (usually not exceeding 10 years). The seller would actually never do that; instead, the company would repurchase the right before it is exercised. These equity "kickers" can provide note holders with total yields in the low double digits, between 10% and 14% in most cases. Returns will always be reflective of the current market. Seller notes are not an all-or-nothing proposition. For example, a bank might finance part of the total package, with the seller note subordinated to the bank loan (and, therefore, potentially having a higher rate of return than if it is the only financing).

This type of financing creates a unique opportunity for both the company and the seller. The company can be the recipient of a financing package that is unlikely to be available through commercial banks. The seller gets a rate of return that is better than what could normally be obtained in other interest-bearing investments. The company can leave its relationship in place with the bank so that it continues to retain working capital lines of credit as well as other forms of capital for growth. The noteholder will, of course, need to subordinate its interest to that of its bank. The seller can also defer taxation on the gains made from the sale, as described in the chapter on using the Section 1042 tax-deferred "rollover" that appears later in this book.

There are negatives in providing seller financing: limited or no immediate liquidity, the risk of loss of principal, and the need to remain tied to the business if a full exit is desired. However, the positives of reducing the lead time for the transaction, lower transaction costs, repayment flexibility should cash flow issues arise, and achieving a fixed income component with market-level returns can be very appealing to sellers.

Much has been written about the use of assets in existing retirement plans to partially fund a leveraged ESOP to reduce the amount of debt required to complete a transaction. Often, in closely held businesses the shareholders themselves function as trustees of 401(k) and profit-sharing plans. The idea of converting a portion of those assets into "equity" in a leveraged ESOP is difficult from a fiduciary standpoint. Keep in mind that they are selling shareholder-trustees of these retirement plans; as fiduciaries, they are acquiescing to the use of funds that are currently invested in a wide variety of debt and equity instruments that will now be invested in employer securities. This creates not only a fiduciary concern but also perhaps an elimination of an employee benefit. There have been cases involving existing retirement plans where a portion of those plans' assets have been converted to an ESOP. Although no one has indicated what might soften fiduciary responsibility when a selling shareholder is a trustee, there may be a conflict-of-interest concern if a shareholder-trustee uses more than 10% to 20% of the retirement plan assets in a new leveraged ESOP. It should also be noted that since you are asking the participants of diversified qualified retirement plans to shift their assets to this concentrated employer security plan, significant financial disclosure will need to be made in order for plan participants to make a sound investment decision. This is not particularly palatable to most companies.

Many business owners try to accomplish as much as possible in a first-phase transaction. A very viable alternative is to scale back the size of the initial transaction to ease cash flow concerns. This also allows the company to continue growing even if the thought of leverage scares the business owner. Another possibility is for the company to initiate an unleveraged ESOP in which contributions for purchasing any employer's securities can be made. This allows the company to begin setting aside monies for the actual stock purchase at a later date. Then, when the selling shareholder is ready, the stock can be purchased either on an unleveraged basis, or on a leveraged basis that uses less debt than would be necessary on an unleveraged basis.

Conclusion

Leveraged ESOPs are viable alternatives as exit strategies. This form of recapitalization has excellent tax advantages not only for selling shareholders, but also for the company sponsoring the plan. The ability to pay back loans with pretax dollars is a tremendous advantage in any type of leveraged buyout. It is important, however, that a financial advisor structure the transaction so it does not encumber the business in a way that inhibits future growth. Structured properly and with great care to allow for amortizing the loan satisfactorily, the leveraged ESOP is a powerful tool in managing the transition of a business to the next generation, thus providing effective business succession planning.

Chapter 5

ESOP Feasibility

Ronald J. Gilbert and Paige A. Ryan

Whenever the subject of ESOP feasibility is discussed, the following basics will always or should always be examined:

- Is the valuation acceptable to the selling shareholder(s) and to the ESOP trustee or ESOP committee?

- Will the cash flow of the company support the debt needed to acquire the block of stock being offered to the ESOP as well as future capital needs?

- Can the divergent interests of various shareholders be accommodated through the ESOP?

- Will the repurchase obligation costs associated with the buyback of stock from departing ESOP participants in a closely held company be manageable?

- At what level of ESOP ownership are current shareholders comfortable?

- Will the corporate governance issues, including a vote pass-through in certain instances, be acceptable to current controlling shareholders?

- Will the required ESOP contributions fall within the allowed limitations?

In addition to these basic items, we recommend that a number of other factors be examined in a feasibility study to identify red flags early in the process, which may indicate that an ESOP is not feasible or that a better option exists.

Tax Benefits

ESOPs often provide substantial tax advantages to the company, selling shareholders, and employees.

Tax-Deductible Principal Repayment[1]

Contributions used to make ESOP loan principal payments are tax-deductible to the corporation.

Tax-Free S Corporation Income[2]

Income attributable to stock owned by an S corporation ESOP is not subject to federal tax. This benefit may not be available for companies with approximately 12 or fewer employees, due to Code Section 409(p), and may not be feasible for companies with a larger number of employees.

Tax-Deductible C Corporation Dividends[3]

Dividends on C corporation ESOP stock that are "passed through" the ESOP to participants or used to repay ESOP loans may be tax-deductible to the corporation. These dividends are not counted in the normal contribution limit of 25% of payroll.

Contributions May Be Reimbursable Under Federal Government Cost-Plus Contracts[4]

Under certain types of federal government contracts, the company is reimbursed by the federal government for the ESOP contribution. Both cash and stock contributions are allowable costs, and thus are reimbursable. There is no distinction between S corporation and C corporation ESOPs. The Cost Accounting Standards Board (CASB) issued a final ruling in May 2008 that applies to federal government contractors that

---

1. Internal Revenue Code ("Code") Section 404(a)(9).
2. Code Sections 409(p) and 512(e)(3).
3. Code Section 404(k).
4. Federal Acquisition Regulation Section 31-205.6.

sponsor ESOPs. The effective date of 48 CFR Part 9904 was June 2, 2008. It amends Cost Accounting Standards (CAS) 412 and 415, which clarified that the "contractor's cost shall be measured by the contractor's contribution, including interest and dividends if applicable, to the ESOP." The CASB did not use the GAAP approach in SOP 93-6, which measures compensation expense for a leveraged ESOP based on the fair market value of shares released in a year.

Section 1042 "Tax-Free" Rollover Benefit and Eligibility

The major benefit for an eligible shareholder selling stock to an ESOP sponsored by a closely held C corporation is the "tax-free" rollover under Code Section 1042. However, a significant tax benefit is derived only if there is a substantial difference between the basis in the selling shareholder's stock and the selling price to the ESOP. Most shareholders in closely held companies have a low basis in their stock, and thus most of the selling price of their stock is subject to capital gains taxes. The ability to defer this tax by a sale to the ESOP is therefore very attractive. Assuming a long-term federal capital gains rate of 20%, and up to 23.8% with the Medicare surtax, and assuming a state capital gains rate of 5%, this tax benefit would be worth approximately 25% to 28.8% of the selling price, or a minimum of $250,000 for every million dollars of the ESOP transaction. The alternative minimum tax may increase the effective rate.

However, to the extent that the stock being sold to the ESOP had a basis equal to or greater than the selling price, there would be no capital gains tax liability. If the basis were only slightly below the selling price, the amount of capital gains tax would be minimal. Thus, the first item on our "preliminary assessment" or "pre-feasibility" checklist is to look at the basis of stock versus the selling price.

An example of shares that frequently have a basis near the current fair market value of the stock is stock acquired through the distribution from an estate of a deceased shareholder. Thus, children who have recently received stock from the estate of one or both of their parents typically enjoy little or no tax benefit from selling that stock to an ESOP. If the "tax-free" rollover is elected, and the qualified replacement property (bonds or stocks of U.S. operating corporations) is held until death, the estate, under current tax law, receives a "stepped up" basis at death. The effect is that the capital gain tax is extinguished. In this scenario, the capital gains tax is never paid.

Eligibility

• Stock with a holding period of less than three years, stock acquired in a certain manner, stock of publicly traded companies, S corporation stock, and "Section 83b" stock is not eligible for tax-free rollover treatment.

• Stock acquired in connection with employment is generally not eligible for tax-free rollover treatment. An example would be stock purchased by an employee through a corporate-sponsored stock option program. Stock distributed from a retirement plan, such as a 401(k) plan or an ESOP, also is ineligible for tax-free rollover treatment.

• If the corporation is publicly traded, its stock is ineligible for tax-free rollover treatment. This includes stock listed on the New York Exchange, AMEX, or NASDAQ. Even being listed on an electronic exchange may make the shares ineligible for tax-free rollover treatment. The corporation is also an ineligible shareholder for the tax-free rollover.

• Only voting common stock with the highest dividend rights or convertible preferred that is convertible into voting common stock with the highest dividend rights is eligible to be sold for tax-free rollover treatment.

If, however, a shareholder holds stock that is ineligible for "tax-free" rollover treatment, it may be possible to have a tax-free recapitalization that converts the existing ineligible stock (nonvoting common, straight preferred, etc.) into eligible stock. The details that determine whether such a recapitalization can be accomplished on a tax-free basis go beyond the scope of this chapter. However, shareholder approval of such recapitalization is normally required. If such a tax-free recapitalization can be accomplished, the holding period of the old security prior to conversion is "tacked on" and can be used to satisfy the three-year holding period required for tax-free rollover treatment. It is not necessary to start the "holding period" clock over again after a conversion.

If the selling shareholder who is eligible for "tax-free" rollover treatment elects this treatment and the sponsoring company consents to the treatment, then certain shareholders are prohibited from receiving ESOP allocations on any stock subject to the tax-free rollover election. This group of stockholders includes selling shareholders, their immediate family members, and any more-than-25% shareholders. There is a one-year "look back" in determining this percentage. Furthermore, attribution rules apply. For example, the son of a shareholder owning 75% of the company's stock is deemed to own 75% of the company stock by attribution; thus, he is ineligible to receive ESOP allocations on stock sold to the ESOP if the seller of that stock made the tax-free rollover election. There is a narrow exception that allows family members to receive ESOP allocations, but the exception does not apply to the attribution rules. Hence, in most cases family members end up being excluded completely from receiving ESOP allocations.

In smaller companies, especially those with a heavy concentration of family member employees, this allocation prohibition may be a reason for selling shareholders to pay capital gains tax on the sale to the ESOP. If this occurs, sellers and family members may then receive allocations of stock in the ESOP, and the ESOP allocations would over time "make up" for some of the capital gains tax that was paid. Without the participation of family members, the covered payroll eligible to receive allocations may be reduced to such a low level that it would not be possible to make the necessary contributions to repay ESOP debt without substantially exceeding the ESOP contribution limits.

The exclusion of certain shareholders from ESOP allocations is not normally a problem in larger companies. To the extent that the corporation would want to make these excluded shareholders whole, it could do so through some type of nonqualified deferred compensation agreement or cash-bonus program that would provide the excluded employee with a future benefit equal in value to the benefit that would have been allocated under the ESOP.

Post-Transaction Decrease in Value

Another issue to be addressed with a leveraged ESOP is the so-called "post-deal drop" in value. In most ESOP transactions, the per-share value of the stock declines after the leveraged ESOP transaction is completed. ESOP appraisers recognize that the corporation then has additional debt and the requirement to service that debt may mean decreased net earnings after the ESOP loan is in place. However, the post-deal drop in value is normally recovered as ESOP debt is repaid. Thus, its biggest impact will most frequently be in the years immediately following the leveraged ESOP transaction.

Financing

The next issue for many ESOPs is how to finance the transaction. Can the company, in fact, borrow sufficient funds to enable the ESOP to acquire stock from the selling shareholders? Funding the ESOP's purchase of shares is the company's responsibility, through contributions and dividends to the ESOP. If supporting the financing burden is too heavy for the company to bear, there are a number of strategies to consider to make the ESOP feasible.

Seller Financing

To the extent that bank financing is unattractive or not available to acquire all of the shares offered to the ESOP, and mezzanine debt is not available or not desired, a frequently considered alternative is seller financing. This means that the selling shareholder holds a note from the ESOP for some or all of the entire transaction amount. If a bank provides some of the debt, the seller note is, in almost all cases, subordinated to a bank loan.

Newly Issued Stock

Another alternative to solving the financing issue is the sale of newly issued stock to the ESOP, which can be in combination with the sale by existing shareholders. These newly issued shares count in determining the percentage of stock owned by the ESOP and thus can be used to partially satisfy the 30% requirement needed for the tax-free rollover. Newly issued shares sold to the ESOP generate working capital for the company, which can be used for expansion, repaying existing debt, etc.

Of course, issuing new shares means dilution. Thus, the current shareholders and the company's board of directors must be comfortable with the level of dilution caused by the issuance of new stock. In some circumstances the dilutive impact can be reduced by the use of a convertible preferred stock, or a "super common" stock in a C corporation, but this also complicates the capital structure of the company.

The ultimate test of the dilutive impact of the new share issuance is determined by the return on capital the company ultimately receives. In the words of a finance professor, "If the company uses the capital productively, the shareholders will be very pleased that they were diluted, but if the company squanders the funds, the shareholders will have quite a different attitude!"

Above (or Below) the Contribution Limit

While it is normally understood that other qualified retirement plans, such as a 401(k) plan, must be taken into account when calculating the 25%-of-payroll contribution limit for ESOPs, there are some other assumptions that are made that may be erroneous.

Interest Exclusion

In C corporations, interest is excluded from the 25%-of-payroll limit when contributions are made to repay ESOP debt. In S corporations, however, contributions to repay interest on ESOP debt are not excluded from the 25% limit.

Above 25%

More than one potential ESOP was almost or actually never created because of a lack of understanding of how contributions significantly in excess of 25% of covered payroll could be made to the ESOP.

As discussed above, interest is excluded from the 25% limit in C corporations. To the extent that 25% is still insufficient to service loan principal, dividends are the answer. Reasonable C corporation dividends can be paid on stock held by an ESOP. To the extent that the dividends are paid on stock acquired with the proceeds of an ESOP loan, those dividends may be used to repay the ESOP debt used to acquire those shares. Additionally, such dividends are excluded from the 25% of payroll limitation and are tax-deductible for C corporations. Reasonableness of C corporation dividends is determined by a number of factors, including industry averages and return on investment. However, if the ESOP owns a convertible preferred stock, or super common stock, the dividend will be determined primarily by the market indicators—for example, a typical dividend paid on similar issues of preferred stock. If, for example, the ESOP appraiser determines that for the preferred stock to be valued at par, it needs to pay a 6% dividend, and the value of the preferred stock held by the ESOP is $1 million, then the preferred stock will pay a $60,000 per year preferred dividend that is excluded from the 25% of payroll limitation.

In addition, the IRS stated in Private Letter Ruling 200436015 (June 9, 2004) that the 25% limit on contributions to repay the principal on a leveraged ESOP's loan in a C corporation is separate from the 25% limit for contributions to other qualified defined contribution plans. (This applies only to C corporations.)

S corporation dividends or "distributions" also can be used to repay ESOP debt. These are not restricted by the definition of "reasonableness," as in C corporations. These distributions are excluded from the contribution limits, which helps a company overcome the 25%-of-payroll limitation. However, S corporation distributions are not tax-deductible. Distributions paid on financed shares may be used to repay ESOP debt. Any cash in the ESOP derived from previous S corporation distributions may be used by the trust to satisfy the ESOP repurchase obligation or to purchase newly issued shares from the corporation. Because S corporation distributions on leveraged stock can be used to repay ESOP debt, ESOP contributions in some S corporations may be considerably less than those required for equivalent C corporation transactions.

Costs

Costs are sometimes cited as a reason not to implement an ESOP. While costs should certainly be considered and understood before undertaking an ESOP, they are rarely a barrier for profitable companies paying taxes, are generally significantly lower than investment banker or business brokerage fees, and in virtually all cases are far outweighed by the tax savings.

The costs of assessing the feasibility of an ESOP, adopting an ESOP, selling stock to the ESOP, and operating an ESOP on an ongoing basis can vary substantially. The variance in fees is driven by the complexity of the transaction structure, the choice of advisors, and the financing structure. Costs are generally broken up into three phases, which include first, determination of feasibility; second, implementation; and third, ongoing costs.

Feasibility Costs

In addition to fees for the ESOP consulting firm, feasibility costs will include the cost of time for corporate executives involved in the analysis. Corporate counsel and CPAs may also participate in this phase of discussion and exploration. A preliminary appraisal is typically obtained to provide a range of value, and this may in some cases also involve appointing an independent trustee. Additional direct costs are associated with engaging an ESOP consulting firm to run a detailed feasibility study, which should include an assessment of cash flow, tax savings, shareholder positioning, financing alternatives, repurchase obligations, employee benefit levels, and to what extent these areas are affected by plan design decisions.

Implementation Costs

This is definitely the area where considerably greater cost is incurred versus other types of retirement plans. Executives today are most familiar with 401(k) plans, for which prototype plans are the norm. Because banks and insurance companies aggressively seek to manage the money of employee participants in such plans, they subsidize other services. Unless such a "subsidy" exists through ESOP service firms providing ongoing recordkeeping services or seeking to fund the repurchase obligation with insurance products, then the true costs of implementing an ESOP will be charged by the practitioners involved in the implementation. As a result, the cost of implementing a typical leveraged ESOP, including an independent stock appraisal, independent trustee, feasibility study, legal documents, and employee communications can approach or even exceed $100,000. However, costs will vary with the experience of the consultants involved, the complexity of the transaction, and sources of financing. Larger and/or more complex ESOP transactions can easily exceed $100,000.

The NCEO's 2015 ESOP Transaction Survey found that transaction costs, including an independent stock appraisal, independent trustee, feasibility study, legal documents, and employee communications could vary from under $75,000 to more than $300,000 (figure 5-1). (A separate chapter in this book discusses the survey results in detail.)

Revenue by transaction cost

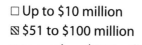

- □ Up to $10 million
- ▦ $10 to $50 million
- ▨ $51 to $100 million
- ▪ $101 to $200 million
- ■ more than $200 million

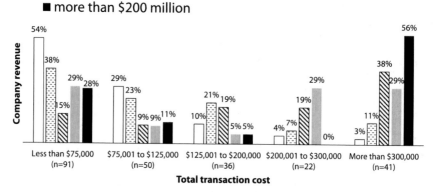

Approximately how much did the transaction cost in total? (This would include legal, administrative, feasibility, valuation and trustee fees, and any other fees associated with the transaction paid by the company.)

Figure 5-1. Higher company revenue is associated with higher transaction costs. Source: NCEO 2015 ESOP Transaction Survey.

Ongoing Costs

Occasionally the "tail wags the dog." That is, companies fear the ongoing costs of operating an ESOP. In fact, operating an ESOP requires the same level of expenditure as operating just about any other qualified retirement plan, including a 401(k) plan, plus an annual independent appraisal fee, and possibly a fee for an independent or directed trustee. Costs for the independent appraisal usually range from $10,000 to $25,000 per year and even more for large or complex situations. However, for most closely held companies, the annual appraisal cost is in the lower end of the range.

The Preliminary Analysis

Many companies considering ESOP feasibility determine rather quickly that it is a "go or no go." That is, they decide, after speaking to one or two advisors, that either the ESOP will definitely work for them or it definitely will not work. On many occasions over the course of the past 35 years, we have seen these assumptions prove to be erroneous upon close examination. Even companies with well-established ESOPs that are contemplating a second-stage transaction will sometimes miss a key point. That "point" can turn out to make all the difference in the world.

A preliminary assessment can be a great first step and is frequently performed on a no-cost or minimal cost basis. Using basic information provided by the company, including projected earnings and a general idea of the ESOP objectives, a one- or two-page preliminary tax-savings and cash-flow analysis is generated. One objective is to quickly identify any red flags that would rule out the ESOP. By focusing on cash flow, it can quickly be determined if there is a reasonable probability of achieving shareholder and corporate objectives with the ESOP.

The Full Feasibility Study

A comprehensive feasibility study of transaction designs provides a decision package for the board and its professional advisors to use as a blueprint for an informed decision regarding the ESOP. Nevertheless, many companies install ESOPs and operate them for many years without the benefit of a comprehensive analysis.

Both the technical and practical factors are measured in the full feasibility study. On the technical side, ESOP contribution limits, the existence of other qualified retirement plans such as 401(k) plans and their relationship with the ESOP, and the company's future status as either a C corporation or an S corporation are carefully examined.

On the practical side, the study conducts a detailed review under multiple scenarios of the company's projected cash flow and its ability to repay ESOP debt, the lenders' collateral requirements, and the projected repurchase obligation of the ESOP as compared with the company's future cash flow projections.

The full feasibility study will also provide a detailed stockholder equity analysis showing the impact on all shareholders such as current sellers, family, and management. It can also examine the impact of various management incentive plans that could interact with the ESOP strategies being evaluated.

The ESOP repurchase obligation is carefully examined and illustrated over at least a 10-year period to cash out vested employees eligible for an ESOP distribution, a practice frequently overlooked by many companies installing ESOPs. These projections for death, disability, retirement, diversification, and "other" terminations can often influence the size of the ESOP's ownership of the company with respect to whether it can handle the ESOP repurchase obligation and still maintain desired growth. The study can show not only comparative transaction structures and sizes but also compare the results of a C corporation versus an S corporation, which often produces widely disparate results because of the different tax treatments of the two corporation types. The ESOP design and implementation should be executed only after careful evaluation of the full feasibility study by the company and all its advisors. The focus of all concerned—as is the case with all well-designed ESOPs—is to ensure the best strategy possible is chosen because it affects the selling shareholders, the company, other shareholders and employees. In many cases, because of the extraordinary tax benefits over several years that are available only to S corporations, the choice will be an S corporation strategy. In other cases, the study will reveal that the size of a desired transaction needs to be reduced after review of the repurchase obligation analysis.

Is an external ESOP feasibility study (as opposed to an internal, or "do it yourself" study) really necessary? It depends primarily on whether the parties making the decision can definitively and authoritatively answer a number of questions.

Below are questions that address most, but not necessarily all, of the important issues that determine the feasibility of an initial or "second stage" ESOP transaction. These issues and the many more outlined below will determine whether or not a company needs an external feasibility study.

Transaction Design Characteristics

1. *Corporate Status?* An ESOP may only be adopted by a C corporation or an S corporation. (There is one private letter ruling (PLR) for an LLC, with very specific facts.) If the company is an LLC, careful consideration must be given, based on tax and legal advice, as to the best method of converting to a corporation.

2. *What is the target percentage of stock for the ESOP to acquire?* This is sometimes driven by the desire of selling shareholders in closely held C corporations to qualify for the Section 1042 "tax-free" rollover, which requires that the ESOP own a minimum of 30% of the outstanding stock of the corporation on a fully diluted basis after the acquisition. Which shareholders qualify for the Code Section 1042 tax-deferred rollover, as well as the need to buy out specific shareholders or to avoid selling stock at a minority discount, also may affect the target percentage to be acquired by the ESOP.

3. *When will the stock be acquired?* Frequently, ESOPs "warehouse" cash contributions for a relatively short period of time before the ESOP acquires stock. However, loan proceeds must be used immediately by the ESOP to acquire stock. Many ESOPs purchase shares in two or three stages over a period of five to ten years or more.

4. *Will the stock be paid for in a lump sum or in installments?*

5. *Will this be a leveraged or non-leveraged transaction?*

6. *If leveraged, what is the preferred length of the loan?* If the ESOP is leveraged (i.e., a loan is made from a bank, another financial institution, a private equity group, the corporation sponsoring the ESOP, or selling shareholders), the lender normally will require repayment over a period of five to seven years. (The company-to-ESOP loan may be for a longer term than the bank-to-company loan.) Some or all of the qualified replacement property (from a C corporation Section 1042 transaction) or other securities may be required as collateral for the loan.

7. *Length of the ESOP loan?* ESOP transactions may be structured through a variety of methods, resulting in external notes between the company and lenders or sellers ("external notes," sometimes called "company notes") and a note between the company and the ESOP (an "internal note" or sometimes called "ESOP note"). With this approach, the company has the flexibility to repay the lender more rapidly if excess cash is available, while maintaining an ESOP note amortization schedule that is amortized by the annual contributions and C corporation dividends or S corporation distributions made by the company. To give the company more flexibility, the ESOP note may be structured over a longer period and should also allow prepayment.

8. *Who sells what percentage?* Where there are multiple owners, if one owner sells first in a leveraged ESOP transaction, the other owners will normally see an immediate decline in their stock value.

9. *Will there be more sales to the ESOP in the future?* Considering the possible timing of future sales to the ESOP following the first transaction may well influence the design of the transaction and duration of the financing between the company and the trust. Future sales to the ESOP can be desirable in that they tend to even out the contributions to the trust and should lessen the possibility of inequitable future allocations of stock to newer employees. The feasibility study may illustrate these transactions.

10. *Which transaction design yields the greatest tax savings?* Accelerating ESOP contributions will reduce taxable income but increase the benefit expense to the corporation due to the fact that ESOP shares will normally be allocated more rapidly to the accounts of ESOP participants. Additionally, for a closely held company, the ESOP repurchase obligation may become larger more quickly when contributions are accelerated. The transaction design with the greatest tax savings is not always the most desirable. Allocating too many shares to participants in a relatively short time frame sometimes leads to an unfortunate situation of two classes of employees—those who were present at the first transaction with large ESOP accounts

and employees who were hired later, after the loan was repaid, with smaller accounts.

11. *How does the transaction design affect benefit policy?* A quicker repayment of the direct or internal ESOP loan means employees at the early stage of the ESOP may get higher levels of benefits than employees at a later stage. By spreading out payments, contributions can be more balanced over time, but tax benefits would be delayed. This is one reason why the company loan to the ESOP is frequently longer than the company loan from the bank.

12. *Is a control premium applicable?* If the ESOP will initially acquire more than 50% of the company's stock or has the option to acquire it within a few years, then a control premium may be applied. A number of factors determine "control in fact."

13. *Will the accounting treatment of ESOP debt cause the company to violate existing loan covenants or create bonding problems?* Generally accepted accounting principles (GAAP) require that the full amount of the ESOP debt be a reduction to the company's book value. Knowledgeable banks will adjust loan covenants.

14. *What is the accounting expense to be recognized by the company when it repays an ESOP loan, and why is it different from the cash expense?* Expense that must be recognized in a leveraged ESOP under GAAP is the fair market value of the shares released from the ESOP suspense account in a given year. The amount of cash contributed by the corporation to repay ESOP principal is ignored in computing the GAAP expense, and the GAAP expense can differ significantly from the tax expense.

15. *Will the accounting treatment of the ESOP debt have an unacceptable effect on bonding, other needs, or loan covenants?* The financial statement impact of the ESOP is of particular concern to companies that are publicly traded, are contemplating an IPO, or require bonding.

16. *Should the company use the fair market value or the cost basis of shares to determine the size of its annual contribution to employee accounts?* The plan can specify either method or can call for using the lower of the cost basis or fair market value.

17. *Cash flow?* A profitable company can normally afford to fund the ESOP purchases because of the significant tax savings involved.

18. *Internal Revenue Code contribution limits?* Contribution limits are normally 25% of covered payroll but can be more or less depending on a number of variables. Company contributions to any other defined contribution plans, such as a profit sharing or 401(k) plan, reduce the contribution limit. This includes corporate contributions but not employee deferrals to 401(k) plans. Interest is excluded from the 25% of payroll limitation in a leveraged C corporation ESOP. "Reasonable" dividends on common or preferred stock in C corporations as well as S corporation distributions also are excluded from the 25% limitation. Other factors affecting plan contribution levels include the allocation basis (see above) as well as allocating ESOP shares to plan participants at a slower rate than would normally occur due to the repayment of ESOP debt. The issue of contribution limits is a complex area that can make or break the feasibility of an ESOP.

19. *Classes of stock?* The ESOP must own either the best class of common stock as to voting and dividend rights, convertible preferred stock that converts to the best class of common, or any class of publicly traded common stock. Convertible preferred or "super common" stock may be used because the larger dividend that can be paid may be necessary due to Internal Revenue Code contribution limits (see above). Convertible preferred stock could be counter-dilutive for stockholders outside of the ESOP. Super common stock is sometimes a viable alternative to convertible preferred stock if an adequate investor rate of return in multi-investor ESOP transactions is a critical issue. As will be seen later, S corporations are limited to one class of stock.

20. *Other shareholder or management concerns?* These could include passing some percentage of stock to other individuals, maintain-

ing a certain percentage of stock ownership in the hands of certain shareholders, or the unwillingness of enough shareholders to sell the ESOP a 30% stake.

21. ***Availability of capital for growth and expansion?*** The debt that the corporation is repaying in a leveraged ESOP can reduce or eliminate any additional debt capacity. As a result, debt capital to expand, acquire other companies, etc., may not be available when needed. As ESOP debt is repaid, shares are allocated to accounts of ESOP participants. This means a growing repurchase obligation for a closely held company. If this repurchase obligation is not properly anticipated and planned for, funds that would otherwise be used for growth and expansion may be claimed by the "buyback" obligations that the company has for participants who retire, die, become disabled, terminate for other reasons (see below), or become eligible for diversification at age 55 with 10 years of participation in the ESOP.

22. ***Who can loan to an ESOP?*** Banks and other financial institutions, sellers, private equity groups, and the sponsoring corporation can be lenders.

23. ***Will warrants be issued?*** According to the NCEO 2015 ESOP Transaction Survey, 27% of ESOP transactions in which seller notes were used had warrants or other stock rights attached to seller notes that were issued to subordinated note holders. These subordinated notes would generally be subordinated to the bank line of credit and other current or future bank financing. Because of the subordinated position, note holders are generally entitled to a higher rate of return. This can be accomplished with a higher interest rate or with a lower interest rate and cash-settled warrants. Cash-settled warrants are typically structured to become exercisable and for payout to begin upon repayment of the seller note. This payout may be structured so that it does not create a second class of stock in an S corporation and so that payments are taxed under current tax law as capital gains. The current rates of return vary based on transaction and market specifics. Companies often issue warrants

with the right to pay out over three to five years at the market rates of interest in effect at the time of payout.

24. *Are other sources of ESOP capital available?* These sources can include the use of the assets of other qualified retirement plans, such as profit sharing plans; wage reductions (or forbearance); or employee investments through a 401(k)/ESOP. All of these approaches introduce a considerable degree of complexity and additional fiduciary risk to the ESOP equation.

Plan Design Details

25. *Who, if anyone, is excluded from the ESOP?* As discussed above, selling shareholders electing the "tax-free" rollover are excluded from ESOP participation, along with certain family members and more-than-25% shareholders. Certain classes of employees and union members may or may not be excluded depending on a number of variables. Employees who are members of a bargaining unit that bargains for retirement benefits may be excluded from participation in the ESOP. (An ESOP, like any other qualified retirement plan, can be the subject of collective bargaining.) Occasionally, small percentages of non-union employees who are in a separate line of work, perhaps in a subsidiary company, are excluded from participation in the ESOP. Any employee with less than 1,000 hours in a year or less than one year of service can be excluded, but there is no requirement to do so. Companies may want to expand the number of eligible employees to increase eligible payroll, which in turn increases contribution limits. In some plans, expanded eligibility may be cut back after a few years if the plan specifies this at the outset.

26. *How can sellers and family members excluded from ESOP participation be "made whole"?* Nonqualified deferred compensation agreements can be used for this purpose. The corporation promises to pay a supplemental benefit to individuals who are excluded from the ESOP. Cash bonuses are also an option. It is important to keep in mind, however, that these cash payments must be reflected in the projections, and may affect the transaction value.

27. **What happens to the following:**

    401(k) plan, if any?

    Section 401(k) plans should be retained—and are by the vast majority of ESOP companies—because they provide a cushion of diversification for ESOP participants and build a stronger retirement position for all employees. Additionally, 401(k) assets are comprised primarily, or exclusively, of employee deferrals.

    Profit sharing plan, if any?

    Discretionary company contributions to a qualified profit sharing plan or 401(k) plan are often shifted to the ESOP.

    Defined benefit pension plan, if any?

    While defined benefit plans are increasingly rare in the private sector, such a plan may stay in place along with the ESOP under certain circumstances.

28. **What voting rights do ESOP participants have?** ESOP participants have very limited required voting rights in closely held companies, but companies can go beyond these if desired. Current shareholders may or may not be willing to share additional voting rights with ESOP participants, such as voting for the board of directors.

29. **Other ESOP plan design features, including:**

    Vesting

    Vesting must be completed in three years (for "cliff" vesting) or six years (for "graded" vesting). Credit is normally given for prior service.

    Distribution alternatives

    Deferring ESOP distributions and/or making ESOP installment distributions over the maximum periods allowed by law will reduce for a period of time the cash necessary to meet a closely held company's repurchase obligation. However, for a company whose stock is growing in value, this policy ultimately increases the cost of the repurchase obligation. Many companies attempt to balance the cash-flow requirements of early distributions with a policy that accelerates to some extent ESOP distributions, especially after some or all of any ESOP acquisition debt has been repaid.

Allocation formula

The "safe harbor" ESOP allocation formula is based strictly on covered compensation, with the current maximum allowed by law for allocation purposes being $270,000 (as of 2017, and adjusted for inflation annually). Alternatives include a formula that gives some credit for prior service combined with additional points for compensation, provided that the formula is not discriminatory.

30. **Do competitors have ESOPs?** If there is a strong track record of ESOP performance in a company's industry, it will be much easier to gauge how to expect the ESOP to perform from a motivational perspective.

31. **Do employees in this industry expect to be equity owners? If so, will what they get from the ESOP be sufficient? Will certain employees need additional ownership?** Many companies provide additional equity incentives to key employees (see question 33 below.)

32. **Are there union employees? If so, will they be treated the same as all other employees or differently?** Union members may generally be excluded from the ESOP. An ESOP, like all other qualified retirement plans, is subject to collective bargaining. See question 25 above.

Management Incentives

33. **Will there be additional stock incentives for management? If so, will such incentives take the form of stock options, a stock bonus, a stock purchase plan, stock appreciation rights (SARs), restricted stock, or a combination of one or more of the above?** Frequently, an ESOP is paired with one or more of these equity-based incentive plans to maximize equity incentives for key

employees. Will any of these incentives create a failure of the anti-abuse provisions under Code Section 409(p) and the regulations issued by the IRS related to S corporation ESOP companies? See question 57 below.

34. ***What other nonqualified plans (such as nonqualified deferred compensation) will be coordinated with the ESOP?*** The existence of the ESOP does not prevent the company from continuing existing nonqualified plans or implementing new ones. Nonqualified deferred compensation plans are sometimes implemented to cover those that are excluded under the Section 1042 "tax-free" rollover rules.

35. ***What is the long-term impact of dilution, if any, of synthetic equity plans?*** By definition, dilution occurs any time new stock is issued. These "synthetic equity plans," such as stock appreciation rights (SARs) or phantom stock, can be value-dilutive because they reduce company earnings. The impact on the per-share value of the stock due to the impact of these plans should be carefully considered.

Fiduciary and ESOP Management Issues

36. ***Will the ESOP trustee be "internal"?*** The board of directors can appoint an internal trustee (but someone other than one of the sellers) for an ESOP transaction. According to the NCEO 2015 ESOP Transaction Survey, approximately 56% of the respondents used an outside institutional trustee or outside individual trustee for the ESOP transaction. Various individuals who are stockholders and/or employees can serve as trustees. There are significant fiduciary responsibilities and risks associated with serving as an ESOP trustee that may justify the cost of outside fiduciaries. Potential conflicts of interest can arise, and sellers to an ESOP should never be trustees acting on behalf of the ESOP at the time when the ESOP transaction is consummated.

37. ***If external, will the ESOP trustee be independent or directed?*** An outside trustee may be directed as to the voting of the shares held in trust. An ESOP committee that may be appointed by the board,

elected in some manner, or formed by some combination of the two would direct the trustee as to the voting of the shares in the ESOP. Both the trustee and the ESOP committee bear fiduciary responsibility unless an independent fiduciary is directing them.

38. *If independent, will the trustee serve for the transaction only or both for the transaction and on an ongoing basis?* Independent ESOP trustees may be appointed by the board of directors for a specific ESOP transaction, either the initial ESOP purchase of stock, a subsequent purchase of stock, or the sale of stock by an ESOP. Except for these specific transactions, individuals are sometimes appointed by the board to serve as ongoing trustees.

39. *If the trustee is directed, will shareholders/management serve as the ESOP committee?* The ESOP committee, frequently comprised of management and/or current or former shareholders, can direct the trustee as to the voting of shares held in the ESOP.

40. *Completing an ESOP transaction and operating as an ESOP-owned company requires a team of advisors. Who will be the following?*

    • ESOP quarterback

    • Independent valuation firm

    • ESOP attorney

    • ESOP lender (for a leveraged ESOP)

    • ESOP third-party administrator

    The quarterback may be one of the other parties listed above, such as the attorney, but frequently is a separate advisor.

41. *What role will the following professional advisors play in the process?*

    • Corporate attorney

    • Personal attorney

    • Corporate accountant

    • Personal accountant

- Personal financial advisor

- Personal estate planning attorney

- Insurance agent

- Investment banker

- Benefit consultant

- Other key advisors

42. ***Who will prepare the ESOP communications plan?*** Announcing an ESOP should be a special celebration. Many companies take employees off-site or have the meetings held after hours. Remote office locations are a special challenge. Recording and distributing a DVD, conducting a webinar, and videoconferencing are frequently used tools. Ongoing communications should be contemplated to maximize the cultural benefits of employee ownership.

43. ***When and where will employee communications occur?*** Announcing an ESOP should be a special celebration with spouses in attendance if possible. Many companies take employees off-site or have the meetings held after hours. Remote office locations are a special challenge. Recording and distributing a DVD, conducting a webinar, and videoconferencing are frequently used tools.

The ESOP Repurchase Obligation

44. ***What are the repurchase obligation projections for death, disability, retirement, diversification, and "other" terminations for the next 10 to 15 years?*** As discussed above, a careful study of this obligation often influences the percentage of ownership of the company by the ESOP.

45. ***Can the company handle the obligation and still maintain desired growth?*** Too large a repurchase obligation in proportion to available cash flow can stifle a company's ability to grow and compete in the long term.

46. *Is the percentage of distributions to "other" terminations—i.e., those who quit or are fired—too high?*

    If yes, what measures will reduce this problem?

    Proper design of ESOP eligibility criteria, such as entry age and vesting schedules and a deferred and/or installment distribution policy, can assist, but the root problem may require careful study of the company's retention system.

47. *How can the cost of the repurchase obligation be managed and deferred?* An ESOP company must adopt a distribution policy. The policy can defer the payout from one to five years depending on the reason for terminations. This "smooths" cash flow and precludes a situation wherein employees with large ESOP accounts are tempted to "take the money and run." The ESOP rules pertaining to "other" terminations allow companies to wait five years before payments must begin, and then balances can be paid out in equal annual installments over a five-year period. However, if a company's stock price is rising faster than its after-tax cost of money, delaying repurchases only increases the cost. Thus, the company must balance the need to defer distributions long enough so as not to tempt vested employees to leave to receive a benefit payment against the need to begin the payout process soon enough to reduce the long-term costs.

48. *Will the repurchase obligation be funded? If so, how and when?* Many closely held companies will fund their repurchase obligations from annual cash flow by contributing, on a tax-deductible basis, the necessary cash to the ESOP in order to distribute cash to departing participants. This approach relies on the uncertainty of future cash flow. It also causes the ESOP repurchase obligation to grow as the repurchased shares are allocated to the remaining participants' accounts. This can create problems for established ESOP companies in which two classes of ESOP participants emerge: some with large stock account balances and some with small stock account balances.

    The decision in a given year whether to have the corporation redeem departing participant shares or recycle shares within the

ESOP has long-term implications of counter-dilution for the non-ESOP shareholders, taxes to the company, and the ultimate size of the ESOP. A detailed analysis of stockholder equity and ESOP repurchase obligation in the full feasibility study quantifies the differences.

A corporate funding plan that establishes reserves on the balance sheet to address this obligation is a wise decision—the sooner, the better. An earmarked corporate investment account can be established. Professional management should be considered for accounts in excess of $1 million. Properly structured life insurance programs have been used effectively by some companies. These funds should be retained in the company, as opposed to the ESOP, for several reasons, including the fact that it may be necessary for the company to occasionally use them for other purposes.

Having a professionally managed cash reserve fund in the corporation is another option that many companies use.

In S corporations, as explained in the next section, there may be a buildup of cash resulting from tax savings and other distributions into the trust that will greatly facilitate ESOP repurchase planning.

Special S Corporation ESOP Considerations

49. *What is the long-range impact of tax savings in an S versus C corporation ESOP?* Analysis has shown that the long-term tax savings generated by S corporation ESOP companies can be significantly greater than for some C corporations.

ESOPs in S corporations currently offer no Section 1042 tax deferred sale opportunity and are subject to reduced limits on the tax-deductible amounts that can be contributed to the ESOP. However, these drawbacks are mitigated by several factors. Because the ESOP's portion of stock owned in an S corporation is exempt from federal (and most state) income taxes, a profitable company may use these savings to make ESOP distributions to the trust that are not restricted by "reasonableness." This will often offset the lower deductible limits and can result in an ESOP loan being repaid faster than for a C corporation. In some companies, large ESOP accounts for selling shareholders will offset a significant portion of Section 1042 sale tax savings.

50. *How much, if any, of company income must be distributed to the ESOP?* The ESOP must receive its proportional share of all S corporation distributions made to shareholders.

51. *What may the ESOP trustee do with cash that accumulates in the trust?* The ESOP trustee may use these funds for the acquisition of more ESOP shares, either from the company (to create capital) or from shareholders, and/or to satisfy the ESOP repurchase obligation. Cash payments to participants through the ESOP resulting from S corporation distributions are not a viable option under current tax law. In addition to being subject to ordinary income tax, there is an illogical 10% excise tax on such cash S distributions made to ESOP participants.

52. *How can these funds promote company and shareholder objectives?* A carefully developed plan can maximize the use of savings in a manner that will balance the sometimes-competing objectives between different shareholders.

53. *What will be the future value of the shareholders' accumulated adjustment accounts (AA account)?* A desirable benefit of the S corporate structure is that shareholders retain individual accumulated adjustment accounts that represent their share of retained earnings on which they have already paid taxes. Since the board may make pro-rata distributions to shareholders at any time, on a tax-free basis, it is important to track the value of these accounts for major shareholders as part of the long-term stockholders' equity analysis.

54. *Will stock be voting and/or nonvoting?* S corporations are restricted to one class of stock. However, with proper design, it may be possible to permit both voting and non-voting stock to achieve particular objectives of the shareholder(s) and the corporation.

55. *What are the effects of the built-in gains and last-in, first-out (LIFO) recapture taxes compared to the tax savings available to S corporation ESOPs?* Depending upon a particular corporation's accounting methods and if and when the C corporation is sold, making the S election may not result in significant additional taxes.

A thorough multi-year stockholder equity analysis will illustrate whether the special tax savings available to an S corporation will outweigh these costs.

56. *What are the implications of the selected plan on the possibility of creating two categories of employees over the long term, i.e., the "haves" and the "have-nots"?* Due to the special features and tax savings associated with S corporation ESOPs, serious imbalances could occur in stock accounts among new versus older employee groups if a company does not plan for the long run. Established C and S corporation ESOPs have managed this problem for many years, some more effectively than others.

57. *What is the impact of Section 409(p) "anti-abuse" S corporation rules?* While S corporation ESOPs enjoy immense tax benefits, these come with increased regulation. These regulations include a test that incorporates "anti-abuse" rules under Section 409(p) of the Internal Revenue Code. These rules attempt to ensure that the regulatory intent of ESOPs, the diversification of wealth by creating broad-based employee ownership, is achieved. The test includes most nonqualified equity compensation, and includes but is not limited to warrants, options, stock appreciation rights, and Section 409A deferred compensation arrangements. Before implementing the ESOP, an experienced third-party administrator needs to run this 409(p) test. On an ongoing basis, the third-party administrator should run the test as needed to ensure ongoing compliance. The 409(p) test must be complied with each day of the year, and it is important to emphasize that 409(p) testing is critical to the success of an S corporation ESOP.

The complete answers to most of the questions above relating to S corporations can come only from a comprehensive financial analysis.

Creating an Ownership Culture

58. *What is the importance of creating an ownership culture in an employee-owned company?* Although the answers to the above

questions are important, the question pertaining to how well the management-employee team is creating a culture change within the organization may provide the biggest payoff to ESOP companies. Some companies install an ESOP primarily for financial reasons, such as a tax-deferred sale for shareholders and tax-favored financing for the company. Many of these companies never develop the partnering message of the risks and rewards to complement the rights and responsibilities of stock ownership. Research indicates that those companies that have effectively communicated employee ownership—thereby creating and enhancing an ownership culture among employees—have reaped the greatest success from their ESOP strategy.

Most ESOP companies eventually make some progress in communicating the impact of employee ownership. However, stellar ESOP companies achieve their full potential by creating a long-term ownership culture, stimulating creativity and innovation among all participants. The psychological reward for employees whose personal innovations and ideas have been recognized by all to improve the organization is quite immediate and contagious.

Conclusion

Once you have answered all the above-listed questions, plus some others that your corporate attorney, accountant, or other key advisor(s) will raise, you may be ready to move forward with implementing an ESOP! Many shareholders, board members, and key management individuals have found the best approach to answer these critical questions is to engage a specialist to conduct a detailed feasibility study that will provide a "decision package" regarding an ESOP strategy or transaction that will truly facilitate shareholder, company, board, and management objectives.

Chapter 6

Investing After You Sell Your Business to an ESOP

Christopher J. Clarkson and Stacie Jacobsen

To the owner of a successful business, the company represents much more than a workplace: it is his or her life's work. Hence, the decision to sell is often fraught with emotion. Sellers may struggle with issues such as ceding control, preserving their legacy, or deciding what to do each morning.

A host of financial issues add to sellers' uncertainty. Business owners who have relied on the relatively stable earnings of their private companies must now live off the far less predictable returns from the capital markets. Ultimately, how sellers choose to invest may make the difference between success and failure in meeting their goals and securing their financial future.

In this chapter, we explore the key tax and investment planning questions faced by sellers to an employee stock ownership plan (ESOP)[1] and provide a framework for making thoughtful decisions by examining a hypothetical case similar to several we have encountered and answering the hypothetical clients' questions.

Essential Facts of the Case

John and Jane, a 64-year-old married couple in Los Angeles, are in the process of selling their business so that they can retire. Their company

---

1. The authors work in Bernstein's Wealth Planning and Analysis Group. Bernstein does not provide tax, legal, or accounting advice. In considering this material, you should discuss your individual circumstances with professionals in those areas before making any decisions.

has produced stable profits, benefiting from a committed management team and hardworking employees. John initially considered selling to a strategic buyer, but he decided not to because many employees would have lost their jobs. Eventually, his strong desire to reward employees led John to sell the company to them through an ESOP.

Sales to ESOPs sometimes occur in stages, often with the seller financing part of the deal by accepting a note. For the sake of simplicity, however, we assume that John and Jane are selling 100% of the business to the ESOP for $10 million in cash.

Like many business owners, John and Jane have long dedicated most of their financial resources to building the company. Over the years, however, they managed to save around $1 million in liquid assets, including $600,000 in qualified retirement accounts through the company's 401(k) plan. They would like to spend around $225,000 per year after taxes and inflation in retirement. Only a portion of that budget will be covered by Social Security when they turn 66.

The couple has one adult child who has a successful career outside the business. John and Jane were generous with his education but aren't overly concerned about maximizing his inheritance. They've discussed leaving something to charity in their wills.

While excited about this new phase of their lives, John and Jane are also anxious about the transition. They have a number of critical questions:

- Will we be able to meet our spending needs?

- How do we choose an asset allocation that balances our need for return with our desire for safety?

- What is a 1042 election, and should we make one to defer tax on the sale?

- If we make the 1042 election, how should we invest the proceeds?

- What are our options for donating to charity?

Will It Be Enough?

For many sellers, the single most important question is the first: "Will we be able to meet our spending needs?" Investors have reason to be concerned: The headwinds to a secure retirement are strong. Increased longevity means a portfolio must last longer: For a 64-year-old couple, there's a 50% chance that one of them will live past age 91.[2] Taxes now take a bigger toll than in the recent past, with the highest federal tax rate for long-term capital gains and qualified dividends at 23.8%, and the top rate on investment income up to 43.4%. State taxes can add as much as 13.3%. Inflation has been dormant for many years but could awaken in the years ahead. And interest rates are now very low, which makes bond investing a challenge.

John and Jane need an investment plan that can withstand these headwinds. To stress-test a plan for long life, high inflation, and poor markets, we use a financial modeling tool that starts from today's conditions and simulates 10,000 plausible paths for the economy, inflation, and a wide range of financial asset classes.[3] From there we determine the probability of various investment outcomes.

We believe a plan should succeed even if markets are hostile and the investor lives a long life. We model 10,000 different futures, and look for plans that would achieve the investor's goals in at least 90% of them. That conservative standard is prudent, in our view.

Defining Core Capital

Our first step in formulating a plan is to determine how much "core capital" the investor needs. This is the amount of capital required to fund after-tax spending needs, through hostile markets, for the rest of the investor's life, even if he or she lives longer than expected.

How much core capital do John and Jane need? John would prefer a conservative approach to investing, so let's suppose they choose to invest 20% of their portfolio in globally diversified stocks and 80% in bonds. In that case, we estimate John and Jane would need a portfolio of $6.7 million today to sustain their $225,000 after-tax spending through hostile markets and a long life. Again, that is a very conservative estimate. If markets are typical, they would leave behind a sizable legacy, even after decades of spending from the portfolio.

---

2. Society of Actuaries RP-2000 mortality tables.

3. This is the Bernstein Wealth Forecasting System, described in a bit more detail at the end of this chapter.

This should be comforting news to John and Jane. The combination of their existing $1 million in liquid assets and the after-tax proceeds from the sale will fund a portfolio well above their core capital benchmark.

How Do We Choose an Asset Allocation?

John and Jane's core capital requirement is driven largely by their age, spending level, and asset allocation. They need a portfolio that provides enough return to meet their spending needs, but will allow them to sleep at night.

For many business owners, choosing an asset allocation is like navigating through uncharted waters. Entrepreneurs build wealth by focusing their expertise and capital in their business ventures. They often prefer to tackle the familiar risks facing their company over the uncontrollable risks of investing in the capital markets. Quantifying the likely impact of their investment choices can help sellers better understand their tolerance for risks beyond their control.

If John and Jane are willing to increase their exposure to stocks to 40% of the portfolio, they could reduce the core capital required from $6.7 million to $6.3 million (table 6-1). The higher expected return po-

Table 6-1. Trading off risk and return for three asset allocations			
Asset allocation	20% stocks/80% bonds	40% stocks/60% bonds	60% stocks/40% bonds
Required core capital	$6.7 million	$6.3 million	$5.9 million
Median wealth: year 30	$8.8 million	$11.7 million	$14.6 million
Probability of peak-to-trough loss >= 20%	2%	16%	47%

Projections are based on the Bernstein Wealth Forecasting System as of September 30, 2014. See *Notes on Bernstein Wealth Forecasting System* at the end of this chapter.

Median wealth values assume the seller pays federal and California state long-term capital gains tax on the sale of the company to the ESOP. See the discussion later in this chapter regarding the ability to defer tax under Internal Revenue Code Section 1042.

Data do not represent past performance and are not a promise of actual future results or a range of future results.

tential of stocks would allow them to meet their needs with a smaller nest egg while building a greater legacy. By year 30, when John and Jane turn 94, we estimate their portfolio would be worth almost $3 million more in typical markets with the 40/60 allocation.

John and Jane might be tempted to pursue even greater wealth creation potential by investing in a portfolio with 60% in stocks and 40% in bonds, but as the bottom row in table 6-1 illustrates, adding stocks increases the risk of sizable losses along the way. Here we define risk as the probability that the portfolio will undergo a peak-to-trough loss of at least 20% at some point over the next 30 years. In our experience, such a large, short-term loss is hard for most investors to tolerate.

While the portfolio with 40% in stocks has a fairly low risk of incurring a 20% peak-to-trough loss, raising the stock allocation to 60% ups the odds to nearly 1 in 2. John and Jane felt this was too much risk for them; it runs counter to their objective of preserving wealth. When they weighed the trade-off between creating a larger legacy and facing a higher risk of a large loss, they embraced the portfolio with 40% in stocks and 60% in bonds.

The current investment environment is challenging, but we believe investors can navigate the landscape by following a few key tenets:

- Adopt a sound investment plan tailored to their needs and circumstances.

- Remember that bonds remain key diversifiers, even though their returns are likely to be low for the next few years.

- Don't abandon foreign stocks, despite recent turmoil overseas. Over the last 15 years, U.S. stocks have outperformed their developed foreign counterparts in seven years and underperformed in eight. Stronger U.S. stock market returns in recent years have left foreign stocks at lower valuations.

- Diversifying beyond traditional stocks and bonds can reduce risk without reducing returns.

- Active risk management and investment selection can help mitigate the impact of challenging market conditions.

What Is the 1042 Tax Deferral?

It is no secret that taxes have taken a bigger bite out of the income of higher earners since 2013. Still, some business sellers are surprised by how much taxes reduce the sale proceeds. The top federal long-term capital gains tax rate is 20%, and the 3.8% net investment income tax applies to gains on the sale of C corporation stock, even if the shareholder actively participates in the business. There may also be state capital gains taxes. John and Jane live in California, where the state capital gains tax rate can reach 13.3% and taxpayers subject to the alternative minimum tax (AMT) can pay tax on gains at a top rate of 37.1%.

Fortunately, selling to an ESOP may allow John and Jane to defer these taxes or even avoid them entirely. Internal Revenue Code Section 1042 provides that owners who meet certain requirements and sell their company shares to an ESOP can defer the capital gains tax on the shares sold to the ESOP.

The rules surrounding Section 1042 are complex, and the seller should obtain the advice of experienced legal and tax counsel, but generally, to be eligible for 1042 treatment:

- The company must be a closely held C corporation.[4]

- The seller must have held the company stock for at least three years before the date of sale.

- The shares must not have been acquired in a distribution from a qualified retirement plan, stock option plan, or any other Section 83 compensatory stock plan.

- Immediately after the sale, the ESOP must own at least 30% of the outstanding stock and must adhere to rules limiting the allocation of that stock to the seller, family members, and more-than-25% shareholders.

John and Jane are clearly eligible for a 1042 tax deferral. Now, they must meet some additional requirements to defer the tax on the sale:

---

4. While S corporation shares may be sold to an ESOP, they do not qualify for the 1042 tax deferral. In certain cases, it may be advantageous for shareholders to terminate the company's S election status in order to sell C corporation shares to the ESOP.

- The seller must reinvest the proceeds into "qualified replacement property," or QRP, defined in plain English as stocks and bonds issued by U.S. operating companies.[5] QRP does *not* include government bonds such as U.S. Treasuries and municipal bonds, foreign stocks, REITs, and mutual funds.

- The seller must reinvest the proceeds of the sale into QRP within a period beginning 3 months before the date of sale and ending 12 months after.

- The seller must file the appropriate documentation with his or her tax return.[6]

Voila! If they take all these steps, the cost basis from the closely held C corporation shares sold to the ESOP will "roll over" into the newly purchased QRP, and the potential tax from the sale will be deferred at least until the QRP securities are sold. At that point, the embedded gain would be realized. Sellers may be able to avoid the tax entirely by holding the QRP until death, when the replacement property would receive a step-up in cost basis.

The Buy-and-Hold Dilemma

Aversion to paying tax is powerful, so the idea of buying and holding a diversified portfolio of stocks and bonds designated as QRP may be very appealing. After tailoring the asset allocation to meet their risk profile, sellers who invest in QRP typically want to sell as little as possible, in order to defer tax indefinitely.

But applying this strategy to the entire proceeds of a sale is risky: It means maintaining a static portfolio as the market evolves. In 1958 the average company inside the S&P 500 Index could expect to stay there

---

5. Technically, QRP are securities issued by domestic operating companies that do not have passive income exceeding 25% of gross receipts for the preceding taxable year, that have more than 50% of their assets in an active trade or business, and whose securities are not issued by the ESOP sponsor corporation or a corporation under its control.

6. Filings include an irrevocable statement of election, a statement of corporate consent, and notarized statements of purchase of QRP.

for 61 years. Today, the average tenure is down to 18 years.[7] Purchasing a portfolio based on a market index today inherently favors stocks that have performed well in the past—but they may not perform well in the future, as table 6-2 shows. A long-term investor must be able to adapt to the accelerating pace of change in today's world.

Table 6-2. Passive investing in cap-weighted indexes is risky

Date	1980	1999	2006
Component	Energy	Technology	Financials
Share of S&P 500	27.0%	29.2%	22.3%
Subsequent two-year sector performance	−51.1%	−56.2%	−63.6%

Source: FactSet, Standard & Poor's, and Bernstein

Buy-and-hold bond strategies are also risky. Even if Fed tightening is slow, interest rates seem poised to rise in the U.S. That would cause prices of long-duration bonds to decline significantly. While buy-and-hold investors may not be troubled by these "paper" losses, they are likely to be less than thrilled with their fixed coupon payments in a few years, if they have locked in today's historically low interest rates.

An Active Approach to Investing in QRP

There is a technique, however, that allows John and Jane to diversify their portfolio broadly, manage it in response to changing market conditions, and/or spend some of their principal without onerous tax consequences. To accomplish all of this, they would buy corporate floating-rate notes (FRNs) that qualify as replacement property (QRP) and hold them for many years. The couple can borrow against these bonds to fund a liquid portfolio at full basis that can be actively managed without the restrictions of Section 1042. Financial institutions lend against these specialized securities at a loan-to-value ratio as high as 90%, but since the credit crisis, loan-to-value ratios have typically been lower, often in the 75% to 80% range.

---

7.   Foster, Richard. "Creative Destruction Whips through Corporate America." Innosight Executive Briefing, Winter 2012.

The FRNs are highly specialized to serve as both QRP and as collateral for a loan. Typically, FRNs are very long-term bonds with maturities of 30 to 50 years and not callable for many years because the deferred tax becomes due when the bond matures or is called. The interest paid by the bonds floats along with the London Interbank Offered Rate (LIBOR), usually with quarterly resets. The floating-rate coupon keeps the price of the bonds relatively stable and results in increasing cash flows in a rising interest-rate environment (and decreasing cash flows in a falling interest-rate environment).

Most FRNs are issued by highly rated companies and carry put options allowing the holder to sell the bond back to the issuer at close to par value on each anniversary date, if the bond's credit quality worsens materially. Issuers include established companies, such as GE Capital, Procter & Gamble, 3M, UPS, Colgate-Palmolive, and certain banks.

The FRN market is small and relatively illiquid, so it takes time to build a portfolio with even a handful of names. Thus, it is imperative for sellers to begin building a QRP portfolio as quickly as possible after closing the sale to meet the 12-month investment deadline.

The cost of this arrangement is that the FRNs generally pay an interest rate below LIBOR, while the monetization loans typically charge an interest rate above LIBOR. In other words, investors pay a spread or annual "cost of carry" to finance deferral of capital gains tax. Furthermore, at least 10% of the sale proceeds will return only a sub-LIBOR rate, since the banks will lend no more than 90% against the FRNs' value. Finally, transaction costs on FRNs can be significant. Sellers must carefully consider the impact of these costs, especially for sales under $5 million.

The benefit is that they could defer 37.1% in federal and California capital gains tax, potentially forever.

When Sellers Finance the ESOP

For simplicity's sake, we assumed above that John and Jane sold the company to the ESOP for cash, but most ESOP transactions involve seller financing for at least some portion of the deal. This means that the seller agrees to accept payment over time, with interest. While this offers a number of advantages to sellers and makes larger deals possible, it creates credit risk: If the economy weakens or the business weakens for some other reason, the ESOP may not be able to make payments on the seller note. This was the case for several ESOP deals during the recession after the credit crisis of 2008.

Seller financing can also raise practical hurdles to making a 1042 election. Let's say John and Jane provided seller financing for 60% of the transaction and received 40% of the $10 million sale price in cash up front. In this case, the deal wouldn't provide enough cash to purchase $10 million of QRP within the 15-month window to make full use of the 1042 deferral.

But John and Jane could borrow money to buy the FRNs, as in the example above,[8] and repay the bank loan as they receive payments from the ESOP on the seller's note. In this way, FRNs also can help sellers to clear the practical hurdle to making a 1042 election that seller financing erected.

Should We Take the 1042 Deferral?

To help John and Jane evaluate the trade-off between paying the tax and electing to take the 1042 deferral, we project their wealth under both scenarios. In each case, the 64-year-old couple has $1 million in liquid assets, including $600,000 in a 401(k); they sell 100% of the business to an ESOP for $10 million; they have $0 cost basis in the stock; and they want to spend $225,000 per year after taxes.

In Scenario A, they pay the capital gains tax on the sale and reinvest the proceeds in a portfolio with 40% in stocks and 60% in bonds. In Scenario B, they use the proceeds of the sale to purchase $10 million of FRNs with an average coupon of LIBOR minus 0.3%, and they use the FRNs as collateral to borrow $9 million at an interest rate of LIBOR plus 0.9%, for a 1.2% cost of carry. They reinvest the $9 million from the loan in a portfolio with 40% in stocks and 60% in bonds.

---

8. FRNs purchased in the secondary market are immediately eligible to collateralize a loan. FRNs purchased as new issues are subject to additional regulations. The institution selling the new issue FRN cannot lend against the FRN for 31 days. Thus, new issue FRNs must be purchased with cash or funds borrowed from another source.

Table 6-3. An active 1042 strategy can significantly boost wealth	Scenario A: pay tax	Scenario B: active 1042 strategy
30-year wealth in typical markets	$11.7 million	$16.5 million
30-year wealth in hostile markets	$3.7 million	$5.4 million

Projections are based on the Bernstein Wealth Forecasting System as of September 30, 2014. See *Bernstein Notes on Wealth Forecasting System* at the end of this chapter.

Data do not represent past performance and are not a promise of actual future results or a range of future results.

Table 6-3 shows that in either scenario, John and Jane are likely to increase their liquid wealth, even after spending from the portfolio for the next 30 years. If they decide to pay the capital gains tax on the company sale, we project that they will accumulate $11.7 million in typical markets. If markets are hostile, we project that there is a 90% chance that John and Jane will have at least $3.7 million remaining at age 94.

But the active 1042 reinvestment strategy offers a clear advantage. We project that in 30 years, John and Jane will accumulate $16.5 million in typical markets and $5.4 million in hostile markets.[9] Both outcomes are more than 40% higher than the related projection for paying tax now.

To put this in perspective, we calculated the pretax sale price John and Jane would need to negotiate today in a taxable sale in order to accumulate $16.5 million in 30 years (the same wealth achieved by selling to the ESOP). We estimate that they would need to sell the company for $11.8 million before taxes, or 18% more than the $10 million the ESOP would pay, to achieve the same wealth in 30 years.

In our analysis, the benefit of deferring the tax on the sale of the company shares to the ESOP clearly outweighs the annual cost of carry and the cost of investing 10% of the proceeds in a low-coupon FRN. The active 1042 reinvestment strategy essentially finances the tax deferral, while providing liquidity and freedom to manage the capital. At this transaction size, we think it's wise to make use of the 1042 election and deferral, when possible.

---

9. This assumes the FRNs are held for the entire 30 years and receive a step-up in cost basis when John and Jane die. If they sell the FRNs, the embedded capital gains tax comes due.

What Are Our Options for Donating to Charity?

Like many business owners, John and Jane wanted to share their good fortune with charitable causes dear to them. While working on the sale, they began to wonder what charitable-giving strategies to consider and whether to implement them before closing the deal.

It's wise to raise these questions early. If John and Jane were selling their company to a third party, there would be a material advantage to making the charitable donation before closing the sale. When donating cash to charity, the donor receives a charitable income tax deduction for the value of the cash donation. For a donor in the 40% income tax bracket, donating $10,000 would save $4,000 in income tax, reducing the effective cost of the donation to $6,000. But if the donors give company shares with a cost basis of 0, they also avoid the embedded capital gains tax on the sale, reducing the effective cost of the gift even more.

For a 1042 sale to an ESOP, however, there's typically no advantage to making a charitable donation before closing the sale: QRP with a low cost basis can be given to charity at any time. In some cases it may be advantageous to donate company shares before the sale to the ESOP, especially if the shares are ineligible for 1042 treatment. Sellers should not contribute the shares to charity on the understanding that the ESOP will buy the stock at a prearranged price, because the ESOP trustees can't be compelled to do so. It's important to discuss these issues with qualified tax and legal counsel.

For John and Jane, the issue wasn't the timing of the gift, but the best vehicle to use. They considered two vehicles that are attractive today and would potentially fit their situation: a donor-advised fund and a charitable remainder trust.

A donor-advised fund is an account that the donor creates with a sponsoring charitable organization. The donor funds the account with cash or securities that can be sold and reinvested in a tax-free environment. Over time, the donor uses these funds to make grants to charities. The donor-advised fund can be an excellent way to pre-fund charitable gifts the donor intends to make over the next many years, while receiving an income tax deduction today.

In a charitable remainder trust (CRT), by contrast, the donor contributes low-basis assets to a trust that can sell and reinvest without immediate tax consequences, and the trust makes a taxable distribution to the donor each year. The donor receives an upfront charitable income tax deduction based on the actuarial value of the assets that will pass to the charity at the termination of the trust, which usually occurs at the death of the donor and spouse.

John and Jane chose to use the CRT because it gave them greater confidence that they could meet their retirement spending needs and because it offers very attractive tax benefits.

Today's higher, more progressive tax rates[10] make CRTs more attractive than they have been in recent years. While selling a valuable low-basis asset would almost certainly push business sellers into the top bracket, a CRT can spread this gain over many years of distributions. As California taxpayers, John and Jane can save nearly $80,000 in tax by running $1 million of realized capital gains "through the brackets," instead of paying top marginal rates.[11]

To estimate how much the CRT would help John and Jane, we assumed that they sell the $10 million business to the ESOP and make a 1042 election, choose the active 1042 reinvestment strategy for only 75% of the sale proceeds, and contribute the other 25%, or $2.5 million of low-basis assets, to a CRT. We also assumed that the couple is willing to take more risk inside the CRT than in their personal portfolio to maximize cash flow: they decide to invest 70% of the trust assets in stocks and 30% in bonds. We then evaluated CRTs with three different unitrust payout rates: the 5% minimum, 8%, and the 10.6% maximum allowable for people their ages.

As table 6-4 illustrates, the CRT would increase their median projected personal wealth in year 30, regardless of the payout rate. With the 5% CRT, the personal wealth advantage is quite small, but for the 8% CRT it grows to $1.25 million.

When we add in the trust assets that will pass to charity, the total wealth created with the CRT strategy increases meaningfully. The 5% CRT maximizes the charitable remainder and total wealth created (since

---

10. Joint filers do not reach the top federal capital gains tax bracket until taxable income exceeds $464,850, and the 3.8% net investment income tax does not apply until modified adjusted gross income reaches $250,000.

11. Paul Lee and Steve Schilling, "CRTs Are Back (in Four Delicious Flavors)," *Trusts & Estates* October 2014, p. 31.

		Active 1042	75% active 1042; 25% CRT with 5% payout	75% active 1042; 25% CRT with 8% payout	75% active 1042; 25% CRT with 10.6% payout
Table 4. CRTs benefit the donor and the charity (M = million)					
	Pay tax				
Year 30: median personal wealth	$11.7M	$16.5M	$16.65M	$17.75M	$17.85M
Charity	$0	$0	$4.3M	$1.7M	$0.8M
Total wealth	$11.7M	$16.5M	$20.95M	$19.45M	$18.65M
Years to median crossover; active 1042 strategy			30 years	24 years	21 years

Projections are based on the Bernstein Wealth Forecasting System as of September 30, 2014. *See Notes on Bernstein Wealth Forecasting System* at the end of this chapter.

Median wealth values assume the seller pays federal and California state long-term capital gains tax on the sale of the company to the ESOP.

All calculations of permissible payouts and associated tax deductions for the CRT are according to Sections 7520 and 664 of the Internal Revenue Code of 1986, as amended, and the Treasury regulations thereunder.

Data do not represent past performance and are not a promise of actual future results or a range of future results.

less money goes to the couple). Over 30 years, the 5% CRT produces 27% more wealth than the ESOP 1042 strategy alone, and 79% more wealth than paying the tax on the upfront sale.

A CRT is not right for everyone. The decision to fund the CRT is irrevocable, and it takes time to accumulate greater personal wealth. It often requires two to three decades before the donor's personal wealth "crosses over" the value that he or she could expect without the CRT, as table 6-4 also shows. Still, for the business owner with some charitable intent, a CRT can be a very attractive option.

Tying the Plan Together

After evaluating all of their options, John and Jane decided that the tax deferral benefit of the 1042 election was worth the effort. Despite the annual financing cost, the active 1042 investment strategy is expected to increase their wealth by $4.8 million. They also chose to use some of their QRP assets to fund a CRT, which would pre-fund a charitable legacy and provide cash flows they could use to meet their annual spending needs. Surprisingly, the gift to charity won't come at the expense of the legacy to their son. In time, they will likely accumulate greater personal wealth by funding the CRT.

Selling a business, to an ESOP or otherwise, can be complicated and laden with emotional concerns. For some owners, investing the liquid proceeds is a source of anxiety. Too often, the question of how to invest the proceeds is delayed until after closing. Though a portfolio can't be built until the proceeds have been received, the investment planning process should start much earlier. Critical tax and investment decisions will affect the ability of a transaction to meet the financial objectives of the seller. As John and Jane found, careful planning and quantitative analysis can help maximize the benefit of selling to an ESOP.

Notes on Bernstein Wealth Forecasting System

Bernstein's Wealth Forecasting System uses Bernstein's research and historical data to create a vast range of market returns, taking into account the linkages within and among the capital markets (based on indices, not Bernstein portfolios), as well as their unpredictability. Asset class projections in this paper reflect the initial market conditions as of September 30, 2014. Globally diversified equity portfolios comprise an annually rebalanced mix of 21% U.S. diversified stocks, 21% U.S. value stocks, 21% U.S. growth stocks, 22% developed international stocks, 7.5% emerging-market stocks, and 7.5% U.S. small-cap and mid-cap stocks. Bonds are modeled as intermediate-duration in-state municipals and intermediate-duration taxable bonds.

Chapter 7

Why I Did Not Use Floating Rate Notes as Qualified Replacement Property

Bill Brett

> *Editor's note: We asked Bill Brett, who until 2016 was the president, CEO, and principal owner of Barclay Water Treatment Co., Inc., to explain why he chose not to use floating rate notes as qualified replacement property to facilitate using the Section 1042 capital gains deferral when selling his stock to Barclay's ESOP. NCEO's founder and former executive director Corey Rosen is a member of Barclay's board of directors and knew about Bill's analysis and decision. Floating rate notes are an appropriate tax deferral strategy for some individuals selling to an ESOP, but there are many factors to consider before choosing this option. This chapter presents Bill's decision-making process. Readers should note that neither Bill nor the NCEO represent this chapter as investment advice. Every owner is urged to meet with a qualified financial advisor to determine the right course of action.*

In spring 2016 I sold my remaining interest in Barclay Water Treatment Co., Inc., for approximately $3.8 million in a seller-financed transaction. With a cost basis of just $52,000, I will face a large capital gain. Because Barclay is a C corporation, I have the option of deferring the tax on this gain if I make an election under Section 1042 of the Internal Revenue Code, which requires the seller to invest an amount up to the proceeds of the sale in qualified replacement property (QRP) within 12 months after the sale. At the time of the sale I received 30% of the proceeds in cash. The balance due will be paid to me over ten years as follows: interest payments only during the first five years, principal and interest payments during years six through ten, and, after the seller note has been repaid, an exercise of warrants for a final cash payment based on the then-current appraised value of Barclay's stock.

Receiving just 30% in cash at the time of closing means that, absent having the remaining 70% of the sale proceeds in cash on hand or available from other sources, I won't be able to defer the capital gains tax on the entire $3.8 million transaction. This would appear to make floating rate notes, as described elsewhere in this publication, a logical choice because using long-term corporate bonds purchased on margin enables a seller to defer the entire capital gains tax. However, I've done the math, and using floating rate notes as QRP is not a good strategy for me.

Floating rate notes are long-term corporate bonds (with 30- to 40-year maturities) that typically can be purchased with a 10% cash down payment and a 90% margin loan at an interest cost of LIBOR plus 0.5%. The interest income generated by these notes is typically LIBOR minus 0.5%. Therefore, the net interest expense (carrying cost) for floating rate notes is typically 1.0% but can be as high as 1.5%. Depending on circumstances unique to each borrower, this interest expense may be tax-deductible. However, someone contemplating the purchase of floating rate notes on margin should expect to pay a 1% to 1.25% net after-tax interest expense (carrying cost) each year. That may not sound like very much, but if a seller were to pay this carrying cost for 20 years and then sell the QRP before death, he or she will have paid the full amount of the federal capital gains tax due on this sale and still owe the tax.

It was explained to me that to qualify someone for a margin loan at the above-stated LIBOR interest rates, banks require 15% of the total transaction in "unencumbered equity." This collateral must be cash or near-cash equivalents and will be held in an escrow security account that in today's economic environment would likely produce very little income. As you can see, 25% of the sale proceeds (the 10% cash down payment plus the 15% collateral held in escrow) will be needed to purchase the notes and for collateral for a margin loan with a 1% annual carrying cost. Investing in floating rate notes also involves legal and administrative costs, and often brokerage commissions as well. I've been told that the administrative expenses for purchasing/selling floating rate notes are prohibitive for transactions under $10 million, but I did not investigate these costs. Finally, there is a small, albeit real, credit risk associated with investing in long-term corporate bonds rated single A by Moody's and Standard & Poor's.

For my evaluation purposes, I simply compared the amount of cash available to invest or spend if I used floating rate notes as QRP versus the amount of cash I'd have available to invest or spend after paying the capital gains tax. I did not take into consideration the return of the loan collateral (15% of the transaction) or the return of the cash (10% of the transaction) used to purchase the floating rate notes because these events would not typically occur during the seller's lifetime, and the net present value of this cash diminishes with each passing year.

When viewed in this manner, the advantage of using floating rate notes to defer taxes versus paying capital gains taxes equals 5% of the total transaction. A seller using floating rate notes as QRP has 75% of the sale proceeds available to invest or spend during his or her lifetime, with the remaining 25% of the transaction used to purchase the notes on margin and for the required loan security escrow account. I am a resident of Massachusetts and am faced with a combined federal and state capital gains tax of 25.2% plus a Medicare surtax of 3.8%, for a total tax rate of almost 30%. This leaves me 70% of the sale proceeds available to invest or spend during my lifetime.

To make floating rate notes significantly more attractive than paying capital gains tax, one must earn a relatively high rate of return on the additional cash (5% of the stock transaction) available to the seller who chooses this option. The size of the transaction has no bearing on this percentage. The floating rate note advantage is 5% for both a $1 million and a $100 million transaction.

The modest advantage afforded by floating rate notes must be weighed against the credit risk associated with investing in long-term corporate bonds and the cumulative net carrying cost of the bank (margin) loan should the floating rate notes be redeemed during the seller's lifetime.

My conclusion is that floating rate notes held to the death of the purchaser may be a good choice for elderly individuals who want to pass on to future generations as much of their estate as possible and may also be a sensible approach for other sellers with a shortened life expectancy. However, for relatively young and healthy owners selling stock to an ESOP, floating rate notes appear to be an expensive way to defer paying capital gains taxes and a potentially risky long-term investment. The 1% (or greater) annual carrying cost for the margin loan is a stumbling block for sellers who expect to live another 20 or more years, and the 15% unencumbered cash margin loan collateral could be a deal breaker for sellers at any age.

Chapter 8

The Prohibited Allocation Rule Under Section 1042

Brian B. Snarr

In allowing the tax-deferred "rollover" under Section 1042 of the Internal Revenue Code (the "Code") of 1986, as amended,[1] Congress sought to encourage broad-based employee ownership by providing business owners with a powerful inducement to sell their stock to an ESOP.[2] To make sure this potent incentive promotes the intended goal of employee ownership rather than encouraging tax-enhanced stock transfers to the family members and business partners of the business owners, Congress also imposed the "prohibited allocation rule" now found in Code Section 409(n). As with many rules in the Code, the prohibited allocation rule is not a model of clarity. This chapter sets forth the rule in a format intended to allow the reader to answer the question, "Does the prohibited allocation rule apply in my situation?"

Briefly, Section 409(n)(1)(A) prohibits, for no less than 10 years after an ESOP purchases shares from a shareholder who makes a Section 1042 rollover, any allocation under the ESOP attributable to those shares, either for the benefit of the selling shareholder or for any individuals "related" to him or her. Section 409(n)(1)(B) also prohibits such allocations for the benefit of any participant who owns (or is considered

---

1. Section 1042 permits a C corporation shareholder to sell his or her shares to an ESOP that will own 30% or more of the corporation's stock after the sale and to reinvest the proceeds without recognizing a current gain on the sale for tax purposes.

2. References to ESOPs should be understood to include eligible worker-owned cooperatives.

to own under attribution rules) over 25% of any class of the employer corporation's stock.

When Does the Prohibited Allocation Rule Apply?

The prohibited allocation rule applies only when an ESOP has purchased employer securities from a shareholder who has satisfied the requirements for a Section 1042 rollover. Consequently, when there is only one selling shareholder, the shareholder and any related parties can fully participate in the ESOP if the shareholder does *not* make the Section 1042 rollover. However, if there are multiple selling shareholders, the situation can become more complicated if even one of them makes the Section 1042 rollover. The more-than-25% shareholder rule (discussed below) can prevent even a shareholder who does not make the election from receiving ESOP allocations attributable to the Section 1042 shares.

What happens if a selling shareholder attempts to make the Section 1042 rollover, but fails, for example, where the 30% ESOP ownership requirement of Section 1042 is not met or where the shareholder fails to make a timely 1042 election? The prohibited allocation rule is applicable by its terms only to assets "acquired by the plan . . . in a sale to which section 1042 applies."[3] If Section 1042 does not apply because of a failure to meet its requirements, the prohibited allocation rule will not apply either. If the Section 1042 rollover is partly effective and partly ineffective, the prohibited allocation rule will still apply, because Section 1042 would still be partly applicable.

To Whom Does the Prohibited Allocation Rule Apply? ("Restricted Persons")

This is often the most difficult question in applying the prohibited allocation rule, because the attribution rules widen the nonallocation net to include related parties and persons whose ownership may be constructive rather than actual. The individuals affected by the prohibited allocation rule are referred to in this chapter as "restricted persons."

---

3.   Code § 409(n)(1).

The Selling Shareholder

A person who has made a Section 1042 rollover cannot receive an allocation attributable to the employer securities sold to the ESOP. This is an understandable limitation, given the purpose of Section 1042. The former shareholder has already received such a substantial tax benefit on the rollover that getting his or her shares back from the ESOP on a further tax-deferred basis was considered by Congress to be excessive.

In a 1990 private letter ruling involving multiple selling shareholders, all of whom made the Section 1042 rollover, the Internal Revenue Service (IRS) held that they were all prevented from receiving allocations attributable to 1042 employer securities, even where one shareholder's allocation of employer securities was demonstrably purchased from a different selling shareholder.[4]

However, a selling shareholder who has made a Section 1042 rollover should be permitted to receive unrestricted allocations under an ESOP sponsored by an unrelated employer, provided the prohibited allocation rule does not apply for a different reason (for example, because the shareholder is related to a selling shareholder in the other ESOP or is subject to the 25% shareholder limitation). Also, as discussed below under "Exceptions to the Prohibited Allocation Rule," the rule does not apply to shares as to which the Section 1042 election was *not* made.

Certain Relatives of the Selling Shareholder

Once a shareholder sells employer securities to an ESOP and makes a Section 1042 rollover, the prohibited allocation rule prevents allocations to individuals related to the selling shareholder within the meaning of Code Section 267(b).[5] Only individuals related to a selling shareholder who makes the Section 1042 rollover will be affected.[6] Individuals related to a selling shareholder who does not make the Section 1042

---

4. Private Letter Ruling (PLR) 9041071 (July 18, 1990).

5. Although Temp. Treas. Reg. § 1.1042-1T A-2(a)(3)(ii) limits the prohibited allocation rule to family members under Code § 267(c)(4), the applicable provision in § 409(n)(1)(A)(ii) imposes the rule on a broader range of related persons. This follows from an amendment to the restricted allocation rule in the 1986 Tax Reform Act that is not reflected in the regulation.

6. See Code § 409(n)(1)(A)(ii).

rollover will not be affected (unless the more-than-25% shareholder rule applies to them).

Following is a list of the individuals who are considered to be related to a selling shareholder, as listed in Section 267(b):

- *Brothers and sisters.* The selling shareholder's half brothers and sisters count as brothers and sisters.[7]

- *Spouse.* The selling shareholder's legal spouse, including a separated spouse if there is no annulment or final decree of divorce.[8]

- *Ancestors.* Ancestors include the selling shareholder's parents, grandparents, and great grandparents.

- *Lineal descendants.* They include the selling shareholder's children, grandchildren, and great grandchildren. Legally adopted children are considered children for this purpose.[9]

- *Trust beneficiaries.* Such a relationship exists when a trust sells shares to an ESOP and makes the Section 1042 rollover,[10] and a trust beneficiary is employed by the ESOP sponsor.[11]

- *Estate beneficiaries.* Such a relationship exists when an estate sells shares to an ESOP and makes the Section 1042 rollover, and an estate beneficiary is employed by the ESOP sponsor.

---

7. Code § 267(c)(4).

8. The IRS confirmed in Notice 2014-19, 2014-17 IRB 979 that spouses in a same-sex marriage are "spouses" under § 409(n).

9. Treas. Reg. §1.267(C)-1(a)(4).

10. See PLR 9143013 (October 25, 1991).

11. A trust grantor and beneficiary are not considered related parties for this purpose. There are a number of other fiduciary relationships specified in Code § 267(b), but they should not be applicable in the context of the prohibited allocation rule. For example, the fiduciary (i.e. trustee) and grantor of a trust, and the trustees of related trusts, are considered related parties for purposes of § 267(b). Under § 267, this prevents a grantor from recognizing a loss upon transferring property to his or her own trust and prevents related trusts from shuffling assets back and forth to create paper losses. However, the IRS ruled in PLR 9017008 that where the grantor and trustee are acting for their own accounts (e.g., where the trustee is receiving the property in his or her own name rather than for the trust), as would be the case in an ESOP allocation, § 267(b) does not apply. See also Rev. Rul. 59-171, 1959-1 C.B. 65.

- *Partners.* If a partnership sells employer securities to an ESOP and makes the Section 1042 rollover, any partners employed by the ESOP sponsor will be subject to the prohibited allocation rule.[12] Family members (brothers, sisters, spouse, ancestors, and lineal descendants) of such a partner who are employed by the ESOP sponsor would also be affected.[13]

The prohibited allocation rule applies only to individuals because entities cannot participate in an ESOP. Accordingly, many related-party relationships specified in Section 267(b) are not applicable in the context of the prohibited allocation rule because they apply to entities.

The following persons are not related for purposes of the prohibited allocation rule that applies to selling shareholders:

- *Aunts and uncles.*[14]

- *Nieces and nephews.*[15]

- *Stepchildren.*[16]

- *Stepparents.*[17]

- *In-laws.*[18] They include parents-in-law, sons- and daughters-in-law, and brothers- and sisters-in-law.

---

12. PLR 9508001 (October 13, 1994).

13. Under Code § 267(c)(1), for purposes of applying § 267(b), stock owned by a partnership is considered owned proportionately by its partners. Under § 267(c)(5), stock owned by a partnership and attributed to a partner is considered actually owned by the partner and is attributed to the partner's family members.

14. Rev. Rul. 59-43, 1959-1 C.B. 146. This ruling was based on the identical definition of an individual's "family" for personal holding company purposes in Code § 544(a)(2).

15. *Tilles v. Comm'r,* 38 BTA 545 (1938), *aff'd,* 113 F.2d 907 (8th Cir.), *cert. denied,* 311 U.S. 703 (1940).

16. Rev. Rul. 71-50, 1971-1 C.B. 106.

17. Ibid.

18. *Stern v. Comm'r,* 215 F.2d 701 (3d Cir. 1954).

More-Than-25% Shareholders

Once a shareholder sells employer securities to an ESOP and makes the Section 1042 rollover, the prohibited allocation rule prevents allocations of such shares to any shareholder holding more than 25% of any class of stock of the issuing corporation and certain related corporations. The most significant effect of the more-than-25% shareholder rule is that shareholders who do not sell shares, or who sell shares but do not make the Section 1042 rollover, are still limited in their ability to participate in the ESOP.

A person will be considered a more-than-25% owner for this purpose if he or she owns, actually or constructively under the attribution rules of Code Section 318, more than (1) 25% of any class of stock of the corporation issuing the employer securities that were sold; (2) 25% of any class of stock of any corporation that is a member of the same controlled group as the corporation issuing the employer securities; (3) 25% of the value of any class of stock of the corporation that issued the employer securities; or (4) 25% of the value of any corporation that is a member of the same controlled group as the corporation issuing the employer securities.[19]

There are two times when a person's shareholdings (actual and constructive) must be considered to determine his or her status as a 25% shareholder: first, at the time of the sale to the ESOP (and in the one-year period before the sale), and second, at the time shares are actually allocated to ESOP participants.[20]

In determining whether a person is subject to the prohibited allocation rule because of the more-than-25% shareholder rule, the person's own shareholdings in the employer corporation are, of course, taken into account. In addition, a person must add to his or her actual shareholdings (if any) the shares owned by the following persons specified in Section 318:

- *A spouse.* An ESOP participant must include in his or her shareholdings all shares owned by the participant's legal spouse, including

---

19. A controlled group for this purpose is defined in Code § 409(l)(4), which generally requires 50% parent-subsidiary ownership.
20. Code § 409(n)(3)(B)(i).

a separated spouse where there is no annulment or final decree of divorce.[21]

- *Children.* An ESOP participant's adopted children as well as biological children must be included.[22]

- *Grandchildren.*

- *Parents.*

- *Partnerships.* A member of a partnership is considered to own his or her proportionate share of any stock in the employer corporation owned by the partnership.[23] For example, if A is a 40% partner in partnership ABC that owns 100 shares of Corporation E, A will be considered to own 40 shares of Corporation E. However, stock owned by one partner, although it is considered owned by the partnership, is not considered therefore to be owned by the other partners.[24]

- *S corporations.* The shareholder of an S corporation is considered to own his or her proportionate share of any stock in the employer corporation owned by the S corporation.[25] S corporations thus follow the partnership rule rather than the usual corporate attribution rule.

- *Estates.* Stock of an employer corporation owned by an estate is considered to be owned proportionately by its beneficiaries.[26] This includes persons entitled to receive property under a will or through intestate succession.[27] Thus, estate beneficiaries must include their estate legacies in calculating whether they are more-than-25% shareholders.[28]

---

21. The IRS confirmed in Notice 2014-19, 2014-17 IRB 979 that spouses in a same-sex marriage are "spouses" under § 409(n).

22. See § 318(a)(1)(B).

23. Code § 318(a)(2)(A).

24. Code §§ 318(a)(3)(A), 318(a)(5)(C).

25. Code § 318(a)(5)(E).

26. Code § 318(a)(2)(A).

27. Treas. Reg. § 1.318-3(a).

28. As with partnerships, although stock owned by a beneficiary is considered to be owned by the estate, this does not cause the beneficiaries to be considered to own each other's holdings. See Code § 318(a)(5)(C).

- *Trusts.* A trust beneficiary is considered to own stock owned by a trust in proportion to his or her actuarial interest in the trust.[29] This actuarial calculation is performed under a method prescribed in regulations.[30]

- *Grantor trusts.* A grantor is considered to own any stock owned by the trust that he or she would be considered to own under the grantor trust rules.[31] The same rule applies to any other person considered to be the owner of the trust assets under the grantor trust rules.

- *Employee plans.* Any stock owned by the trust established under a qualified plan (profit-sharing, pension, stock bonus plan, or ESOP) is considered to be owned in proportion to the participants' actuarial interests, under the usual trust attribution rules.[32] The Senate Report to the 1986 Tax Reform Act states that in an ESOP, only allocated shares are taken into account.[33]

- *Corporations.* If one corporation owns shares of an employer corporation, then shareholders of the owner corporation are considered to own stock in the employer corporation only if the owner corporation holds 50% or more (in value) of the employer corporation.[34] When the 50% ownership threshold is met, the shareholders of the owner corporation are considered to own the stock in the employer corporation in the same proportion (by value) that they own shares of the owner corporation.[35]

- *Options.* A person who has an option to acquire stock is considered to have exercised the option and to own the stock that is subject to

---

29. Code § 318(a)(2)(B)(i).
30. Treas. Reg. § 20.2031-7. See Treas. Reg. § 1.318-3(B).
31. Code § 318(a)(2)(B)(ii).
32. Code § 409(n)(1) (flush language) provides that the employee trust exception of § 318(a)(2)(B)(i) does not apply for purposes of the prohibited allocation rule.
33. Senate Explanation, 1986 Tax Reform Act, Pub. L. No. 99-514 (October 22, 1986).
34. Code § 318(a)(2)(C).
35. Code § 318(a)(2)(C).

the option.[36] This includes stock that can be acquired under options, warrants, or conversion privileges, so long as there is no condition or contingency on exercise that has not been met.[37]

Reattribution and Its Limits

In calculating a person's stock ownership for the more-than-25% shareholder rule, the attribution rules of Section 318 require counting the ownership of certain other parties. In calculating the ownership of these other parties, it is necessary to consider not only the shares they actually own, but also certain shares that are attributed to them. For example, if a shareholder's daughter owns 500 shares of Employer Corp. in her own name and is a one-third partner in a partnership that owns an additional 1,500 shares, the shareholder will have 1,000 shares (500 + [1,500 ÷ 3]) attributed to him or her from the daughter. This is referred to as "reattribution," which significantly complicates the job of figuring out who owns what. However, the reattribution rules have several limits that prevent attribution from proceeding *ad infinitum*.

First, many of the attribution rules that might otherwise apply under Section 318, for example, by causing a partnership to be considered the owner of stock owned by one of its partners, are simply not relevant when the only issue is whether an individual is considered the owner of more than 25% of a corporation's stock.

Next, in determining a person's constructive ownership under Section 318, another person's stock can be counted only once for attribution purposes, although it will be counted in the manner that imputes the largest total stock ownership.[38] For example, if Wife owns 1,000 shares of Employer Corp. stock and Husband and Son own no shares, Husband and Son will each be considered to own 1,000 shares attributed from Wife. Although Husband's 1,000 attributed shares would usually be further attributed to both Wife and Son, for a total of 3,000 for her and 2,000 for him, they cannot be counted more than once for any one person because all the attribution is based on the same 1,000 shares.

---

36. Code § 318(a)(4).
37. Rev. Rul. 68-601, 1968-2 C.B. 124.
38. Treas. Reg. § 1.318-1(b)(2).

Finally, due to limitations in the attribution and constructive owner-ship rules of Section 318, there are certain related persons whose stock holdings are *not* considered in determining whether an ESOP participant is a more-than-25% shareholder:

- *Grandchildren.*[39] Although grandchildren are not considered to own stock owned by their grandparents, as noted above, grandparents *are* considered to own any stock owned by their grandchildren.

- *Stepchildren and stepparents.* Unlike adopted children, stepchildren and stepparents are not counted for purposes of Section 318.

- *Brothers and sisters.*

- *Aunts and uncles.*

- *Nieces and nephews.*

- *Cousins.*

- *In-laws.*

Overlap in the Restricted Person Tests

There will often be significant overlaps between the prohibited alloca-tion rule applicable to selling shareholders and that applicable to more-than-25% shareholders, both as to the actual shareholders and as to their related parties. For example, if Father owned 50% of a company's outstanding stock and sold 30% to an ESOP and made the Section 1042 election, he would be a restricted person under both rules. However, if he did not make the Section 1042 rollover (but another shareholder did), he would still be a restricted person because of the more-than-25% shareholder rule. His children would also be considered more-than-25% shareholders because they would be considered to own any stock owned by their father. Accordingly, none of them could receive allocations at-tributable to Section 1042 employer securities from the ESOP.

It is therefore very important to examine both restricted person tests. An escape from one is not necessarily an escape from the other.

---

39. See Treas. Reg. § 1.318-2(b).

To What Allocations Does the Prohibited Allocation Rule Apply?

The prohibited allocation rule does not prevent restricted persons from *participating* in an ESOP; it simply requires that no part of the plan's assets attributable to the 1042 stock be allocated, directly or indirectly, to a restricted person. Thus, plan assets other than Section 1042 stock (including employer stock contributed by the employer to the ESOP) can be allocated to a restricted person. However, the rule also prohibits "makeup" plan contributions for restricted persons. For example, if a restricted person were to receive an allocation of cash in an ESOP proportionate to the Section 1042 stock allocations received by the other participants, there would be an outright violation of the prohibited allocation rule. The legislative history states that the rule extends to all other qualified plans maintained by the ESOP sponsor, so that an employer could not make an allocation of other assets to a restricted person without making additional allocations to other participants sufficient to separately satisfy the nondiscrimination requirements of Section 401(a).[40]

The prohibited allocation rule is not applicable to amounts payable under a *non-qualified* deferred compensation arrangement, such as a stock option plan, a SERP, or a deferred compensation arrangement paid under a rabbi trust or otherwise.[41] However, if the employer corporation made the S election after the sale by a restricted person, deferred compensation would have to be examined in light of the nonallocation rule of Section 409(p). Final nondiscrimination regulations confirmed that reducing a participant's benefits to avoid a violation of Section 409(p) would not prevent an ESOP from passing a safe harbor allocation test.[42]

Exceptions to the Prohibited Allocation Rule

De Minimis Exception for Lineal Descendants

There is a de minimis exception to the prohibited allocation rule for certain individuals who are restricted persons by virtue of being lineal

---

40. Senate Explanation, 1986 Tax Reform Act, Pub. L. No. 99-514 (October 22, 1986).

41. Conference Report, 1986 Tax Reform Act, Pub. L. No. 99-514 (October 22, 1986); PLR 9442015 (October 21, 1994).

42. Reg §1.401(a)(4)-2(b)(4)(iv); Reg §1.401(a)(4)-2(d)(6).

descendants of a selling shareholder. Lineal descendants of a selling shareholder are allowed to receive allocations attributable to (or allocated in lieu of) employer securities sold in a Section 1042 sale where the aggregate amount allocated to all lineal descendants of a selling shareholder does not exceed more than 5% of the employer securities held by the plan that are attributable to Section 1042 sales by persons related to the lineal descendants. Relatedness for this purpose is determined by the same Section 267(c)(4) relatedness test used for the prohibited allocation rule. Because of the absolute 5% cap, any increase in the number of lineal descendants who participate in the ESOP will shrink the permissible per-participant allocation that can be made within the overall 5% exception.

Note: There is no similar exception for persons who are constructive more-than-25% shareholders because of attribution from related shareholders, so the de minimis exception will almost always be overridden by the more-than-25% shareholder rule.[43]

Shares Other Than the Section 1042 Shares

As noted above, shares purchased by an ESOP, but as to which no Section 1042 election has been made, are not subject to the prohibited allocation rule. So, for example, if three 33⅓% shareholders each sell their employer securities to an ESOP, but only two of them elect the Section 1042 rollover, children of the electing shareholders (even though they are constructive more-than-25% shareholders) may receive allocations attributable to the shares purchased from the non-electing shareholder.[44]

---

43. Given the 30% shareholding requirement of § 1042, most selling shareholders will meet the test to be considered a more-than-25% shareholder, unless smaller shareholders aggregate their stock sales to meet the 30% test. Such a selling shareholder's lineal descendants will consequently be constructive more-than-25% shareholders under the attribution rules of Code § 318. The IRS has confirmed that in its view, the lineal descendant exception is almost meaningless (except for 25%-or-less shareholders who aggregate sales to an ESOP) because it does not convey protection from the more-than-25% shareholder rule. PLR 9707015 (November 14, 1996), Internal Revenue Manual Section 4.72.4.5.1(2)b.

44. PLR 9001035 (October 10, 1989).

Section 1042 Securities That Have Been Repurchased

The IRS has also ruled privately that Section 1042 employer securities previously allocated to an ESOP participant that have again become available for allocation after being repurchased from the ESOP participant on termination can be allocated to a constructive more-than-25% shareholder without violating the prohibited allocation rule.[45] The apparent theory of this ruling is that the shares were not "acquired by the plan . . . in a sale to which section 1042 applies."[46] Under this rationale, any restricted person could receive an allocation of employer securities so long as the shares had been "purged" by having been distributed and reacquired by the ESOP in a sale to which Section 1042 did not apply. This would not be the case with unvested shares that were forfeited and reallocated to a restricted person.

How Long Does the Prohibited Allocation Rule Apply?

In the case of a selling shareholder or related person, there is a 10-year nonallocation period during which the prohibited allocation rule applies. If the stock sale in question was financed with a loan that is outstanding for more than 10 years from the stock acquisition date, the nonallocation period is extended until the final ESOP plan allocation is made when the loan is paid off.[47]

In the case of an actual or constructive more-than-25% shareholder at the time the 1042 securities are sold to the ESOP, or during the prior one-year period, the restriction lasts until all of the employer securities acquired in the sale are allocated.[48] In the case of a person who is not a more-than-25% shareholder at the time of the 1042 sale to the ESOP but later becomes one, only stock ownership on the date ESOP shares are allocated is counted.[49]

---

45. PLR 9001035 (October 10, 1989).

46. Code § 409(n)(1).

47. Code § 409(n)(3)(C).

48. Senate Explanation, 1986 Tax Reform Act, Pub. L. No. 99-514 (October 22, 1986).

49. Ibid.

Consequences of Not Meeting the Rule

Disqualification as to the Restricted Person

If an ESOP fails to comply with the prohibited allocation rule and makes an allocation to a restricted person, Section 409(n) in effect treats the ESOP as being disqualified, but only with respect to the restricted person.[50] The restricted person is treated as having received a taxable distribution from the ESOP equal to the allocation. If the restricted person has not attained age 59½, the excise tax on premature distributions will also be applicable.

Because the prohibited allocation is unlikely to be accompanied by an actual distribution from the ESOP that could help meet the resulting tax obligations, a compliance failure will be doubly burdensome to the restricted person affected.

Fifty Percent Excise Tax on Employer

The employer sponsoring the ESOP (or the worker-owned cooperative that consented to the Section 1042 rollover) also bears the brunt of a failure to comply with the prohibited allocation rule in the form of a 50% excise tax on the amount of the prohibited allocation.[51]

Conclusion

Especially during the first ESOP plan year following a stock purchase and Section 1042 rollover, the employer and plan administrator must be wary of the prohibited allocation rule. It is important to examine the related party attribution rules of Section 267 and the constructive ownership rules of Section 318 to determine which ESOP participants, in addition to the selling shareholder and more-than-25% shareholders, might be affected by the prohibited allocation rule. In plan years thereafter, attention must be paid to whether any participant has *become* a more-than-25% shareholder to whom the prohibited allocation rule applies.

---

50. Ibid.

51. Code § 4979A.

Chapter 9

The 2015 ESOP Transaction Survey

Loren Rodgers and Nathan Nicholson

There is very little data available to inform companies on how other companies structure, manage, and evaluate their ESOP transactions. The NCEO's ESOP transaction survey, conducted in 2015 as part of the NCEO's ongoing survey series, was designed to provide companies with context and comparison for their own experiences, including transaction scope, financing, management, and satisfaction with outcomes.

The Survey

I wish I'd had a better understanding of ESOPs in general.
 —Survey respondent

The NCEO collected data on ESOP transactions in an online survey conducted from February to September 2015. Participating companies were offered nominal compensation in the form of a one-time discount on purchase of NCEO publications. This chapter reports on the responses from a diverse group of 240 ESOP companies. Throughout the chapter we also provide selected responses from an open-ended question on what respondents wish they had known going into the transaction process. The 33-item survey questionnaire is included as an appendix to this chapter.

Using the Data

The ESOP transaction survey attempts to fill a major gap in knowledge about the ESOP world, but the results should be analyzed with an eye to their limitations. The survey respondents were self-selected rather than randomly sampled. A likely majority are NCEO members. As a result, the surveyed companies may have certain characteristics in common that are not representative of ESOP companies in general.

Another limitation of the data is that the transactions described by respondents took place at different times within a period that saw major developments in the ESOP field. One example is the June 2014 fiduciary process agreement between GreatBanc and the U.S. Department of Labor (DOL). This agreement had a marked effect on the structure of ESOP transactions; this before/after effect is visible in the survey results and could make conclusions based on aggregate data from both time periods misleading.

Finally, common practice is not necessarily best practice. Nothing in these results should be taken as a recommendation or guideline for ESOP transactions. Anyone considering an ESOP transaction should consult with qualified professionals who have expertise with ESOPs.

Characteristics of Respondents

As discussed above, the surveyed companies are not a representative sample of ESOP companies. Still, many characteristics of the survey sample are broadly similar to the characteristics of the set of all ESOP companies. Figure 9-1 compares the industry makeup of the respondents to that of the ESOP universe as a whole.

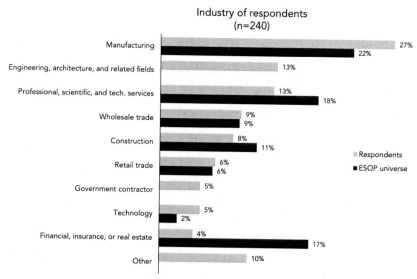

Figure 9-1. Industry of respondents

As with the ESOP universe, manufacturing represents the largest portion of respondent companies. Far fewer are in the finance, insurance, and real estate (FIRE) industries compared to the ESOP universe.

Most respondents had less than $50 million in revenue and fewer than 500 employees. Table 9-1 shows the distribution of revenue and number of employees among respondents.

Table 9-1. Distribution of revenue and number of employees		
What was the amount of your company's revenues in the most recently completed fiscal year?	Number of respondents	Percent
Up to $10 million	69	29%
$10 million to $50 million	100	42%
$51 million to $100 million	32	13%
$101 million to $200 million	21	9%
$201 million or more	18	7%
Total	240	
How many employees do you have? (count both full- and part-time employees)	Number of respondents	Percent
50 or fewer	72	30%
51 to 100	56	23%
101 to 500	85	36%
501 to 1,000	13	5%
1,001 or more	13	5%
Total	239	

Eighty-three percent of respondent companies were S corporations as of the time they completed the survey. Twenty-five percent of respondents reported that the company converted from a C corporation to an S corporation after the initial ESOP transaction.

Respondents tended to be from 100% ESOP-owned companies, as shown in table 9-2.

Transaction Characteristics

In plan design it is very important to consider where you will be and what things you will need 10 and 20 years out. Repurchase obligation and segregation strategies are not on the typical person's radar at the time of the transaction.

—Survey respondent

Table 9-2. Percentage of ESOP ownership			
Initial Transaction (n=135)		Subsequent Transaction (n=96)	
Percentile	Percentage of the company's shares owned by the ESOP after the transaction	Percentile	Percentage of the company's shares owned by the ESOP after the transaction
10th	19%	10th	35%
25th	30%	25th	61%
50th	70%	50th	100%
75th	100%	75th	100%
90th	100%	90th	100%

The survey directed respondents to give information about their initial ESOP transaction or, if the initial transaction was more than 10 years ago and another transaction had since taken place, about the most recent transaction. More than half of respondents (58%) answered about an initial transaction.

The reported transactions tended to be recent, with 47% of transactions taking place in or after 2012. Eleven percent of transactions took place before 2000.

The size of the transactions as a percentage of company equity varied, as shown in table 9-3.

Table 9-3. Size of the transaction		
	Initial Transaction (n=135)	Subsequent Transaction (n=95)
Difference in percentage of company's shares owned by the ESOP before and after the transaction	% of respondents	% of respondents
Less than 10%	6%	25%
10 to 49%	37%	44%
50 to 99%	14%	30%
100%	43%	1%

In terms of dollar value paid to the seller(s), a majority of respondents (54%) answered about transactions of $5 million or less, with most of the remaining respondents (36%) reporting transactions of $5 million to $25 million.

Transaction Context

[I wish we had known] How important it would be to communicate with employees during the process.
    —Survey respondent

These data indicate variation in who initially introduced the company to the idea of an ESOP, with many driven by the owner, as shown in figure 9-2.

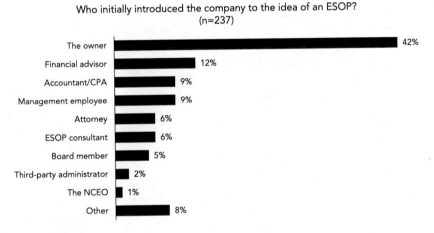

Figure 9-2. Who introduced the company to the idea of an ESOP

Most respondents (83%) did not have a potentially credible offer from another party at the time of the decision to sell to the ESOP. There is a slight uptick in potential alternative offers for more recent initial transactions (20% before 2009, compared to 25% reporting such offers for more recent ones).

Respondents expressed positive attitudes about the impact of the ESOP on their business, as shown in figure 9-3.

Transaction Cost and Financing

Many company-specific factors determine the cost of an ESOP transaction. These include the complexity of the plan, the sources of financing,

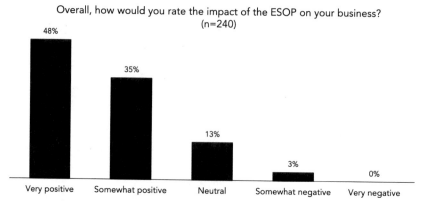

Figure 9-3. Attitudes about the ESOP's impact

the number of parties involved, the need for separate legal representation, and more. On the whole, subsequent transactions were more likely to fall into the smallest cost category, as shown in figure 9-4.

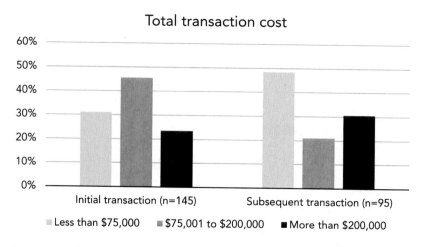

Figure 9-4. Transaction cost

There is a clear relationship between the number of services procured and the total cost of the transaction, as shown in figures 9-5a and 9-5b. For initial transactions, a majority (56%) of companies procuring only one or two additional services beyond valuation reported a total transaction cost of under $75,000, while just 19% of those procuring three or more additional services reported transaction costs under $75,000. For subsequent transactions, a large majority of companies (78%) reported transaction costs under $75,000 when procuring one or two additional services, compared to 21% who reported transaction costs under $75,000 when procuring three or more additional services.

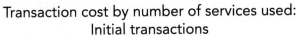

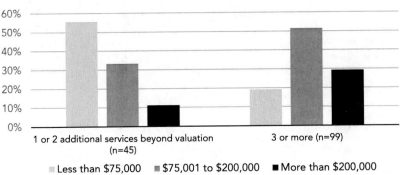

Transaction cost by number of services used: Initial transactions

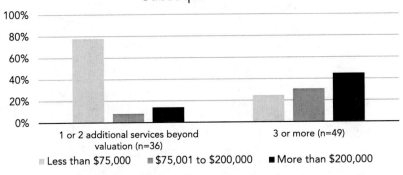

Transaction cost by number of services used: Subsequent transactions

Figures 9-5a and 9-5b. Transaction cost by number of services used

Most smaller transactions (involving less than 10% of total company equity) fall into the smallest cost category, as shown in figure 9-6.

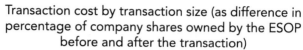

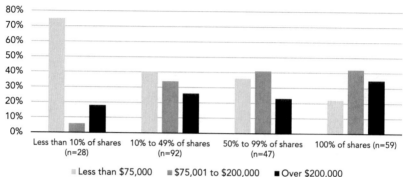

Figure 9-6. Transaction cost by transaction size

More recent transactions were associated with higher costs, as shown in figure 9-7.

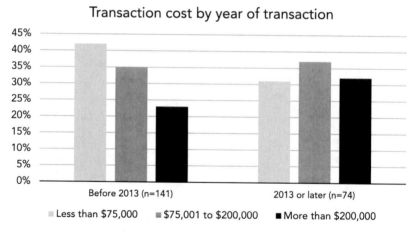

Figure 9-7. Transaction cost by year of transaction

This difference reflects both a long-term trend toward more careful transaction management and an increase in the number of professional advisors. This increase in turn is the result of many factors, one of which is the increased regulatory scrutiny by the DOL's Employee Benefit Security Administration. Perhaps the most important example of this is the 2014 agreement between the DOL and GreatBanc.

Higher company revenues are also associated with higher transaction costs. Figure 9-8 shows transaction costs by company revenue.

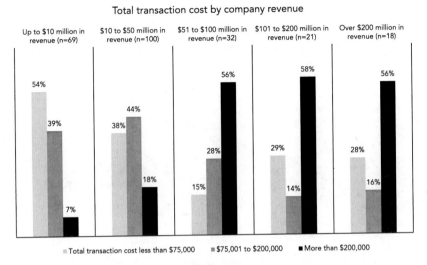

Figure 9-8. Transaction costs by company revenue

Funding

[I wish we had known] That we could have an internal as well as an external loan, so we did not have to allocate all the stock when the sellers' loans were paid off.
—Survey respondent

Most of the transactions included in the data (72%) were leveraged. Of these leveraged transactions, 60% were fully funded by loans. Table 9-4 breaks out the percentage funded among leveraged transactions.

Table 9-4. Percentage funded among leveraged transactions		
Percentage of the transaction that was funded by the loan(s)	Number	Percentage
100%	103	60%
99 to 80%	38	22%
79 to 60%	23	13%
59 to 40%	7	4%
<40%	2	1%
Total	173	

Almost half of the reported transactions (46%) used at least some seller financing. Out of those that did, the seller received warrants, phantom stock, or stock appreciation rights in 27% of cases.

The survey also asked about funding sources other than the seller and third parties. The most common of these was a cash contribution from the company, reported by 39% of respondents. Figure 9-9 shows the breakdown of funding methods used aside from loans.

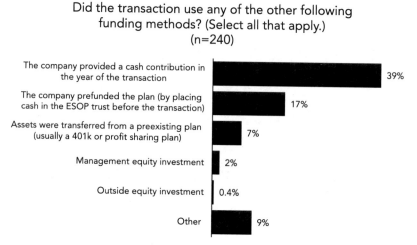

Figure 9-9. Funding methods used

Loan Interest and Term

The median term of the senior note in leveraged transactions was eight years. The median interest rate on loans from an outside senior debt lender was less than 5%, while the median interest rate for loans from the selling owner was between 5% and 8.99%. The interest rate for a seller loan was 9% or more in 13% of transactions involving seller financing.

Deferral of Capital Gains Tax

Slightly over one-third (37%) of respondents reported that the seller took an election under Internal Revenue Code Section 1042, which allows a C corporation shareholder selling to an ESOP to defer capital gains tax if the seller reinvests the sale proceeds into qualified replacement property and meets other requirements. More recent transactions were slightly less likely to involve a 1042 rollover: 40% of companies answering about transactions before 2013 reported using the 1042 election, compared to 30% of companies answering about transactions in or after 2013.

The Transaction Process

The Trustee

An outside trustee should have been named to oversee the transaction to remove the vested interest on the part of the sellers.
  —Survey respondent

Overall, a majority of respondents (56%) reported using an outside institution or individual as trustee for the transaction, 28% a company insider, and 16% the seller.

However, this aspect of transactions has been heavily affected by developments in the ESOP regulatory world. In June 2014, GreatBanc Trust Company and the DOL finalized an agreement laying out new guidance on prudent valuation and fiduciary review processes for ESOP transactions. These extensive process recommendations from the DOL appear to have increased the use of outside trustees in ESOP transactions. As table 9-5 reflects, the use of outside trustees is markedly more common among transactions occurring in or after 2013 than in earlier transactions.

Table 9-5. Trustee types				
Type of trustee	Before 2013		2013 or later	
	Number	%	Number	%
Outside institution or individual	71	51%	48	65%
Seller	25	18%	7	9%
Other company insider	43	31%	19	26%
Total	139		74	

These changes would likely be even more pronounced if there were sufficient responses to show results for before and after June 2, 2014, the date of the release of the GreatBanc/DOL fiduciary process agreement.

Services

We had no surprises, but we spoke with 3–4 companies beforehand and learned that the cost and complexity of the transaction was higher than originally planned.
   —Survey respondent

As expected, virtually all respondents reported retaining valuation services from an outside firm. Figure 9-10 shows the prevalence of other services among respondents.

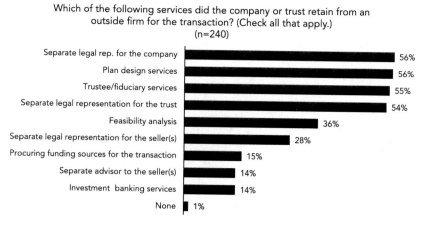

Which of the following services did the company or trust retain from an outside firm for the transaction? (Check all that apply.)
(n=240)

Separate legal rep. for the company	56%
Plan design services	56%
Trustee/fiduciary services	55%
Separate legal representation for the trust	54%
Feasibility analysis	36%
Separate legal representation for the seller(s)	28%
Procuring funding sources for the transaction	15%
Separate advisor to the seller(s)	14%
Investment banking services	14%
None	1%

Figure 9-10. Services used

Figure 9-11 shows the percentage of respondents who reported procuring each of six specific valuation analyses in addition to the mandatory transaction valuation. Supplying a fairness opinion to the trustee and performing a preliminary valuation were both common, but all other additional valuation analyses were used by fewer than 20% of responding companies.

Four in ten respondents reported hiring someone to serve as a project manager for the whole transaction process.

Time to Complete the Transaction

Expect the unexpected. The process was a lot longer than we had anticipated.
   —Survey respondent

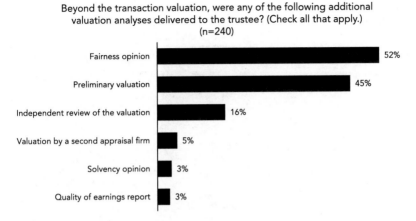

Beyond the transaction valuation, were any of the following additional valuation analyses delivered to the trustee? (Check all that apply.) (n=240)

Figure 9-11. Valuation analyses procured

Nearly two-thirds of respondents (62%) reported completing their transaction in six months or less, starting from when the first letter of engagement was signed with a lawyer or other ESOP professional. Ten percent of respondents took three months or less, and another 10% took 12 months or more. The median time to completion was six months.

Satisfaction with the Transaction

[I wish we had known] all the ways a plan could be designed. We were unaware of all the choices we could have made. The good news is, we got a very vanilla plan and it has served us very well over the years.

—Survey respondent

I wish we had a better understanding of the accounting rules for a leveraged ESOP. We are still learning into the third year of the plan.

—Survey respondent

The survey asked respondents to express their satisfaction with the transaction process overall and with each of several aspects of the transaction. Nearly all respondents (93%) were at least somewhat satisfied with the overall transaction. Very few respondents reported dissatisfaction with any aspect of the transaction asked about in the survey. Figure 9-12 summarizes the responses.

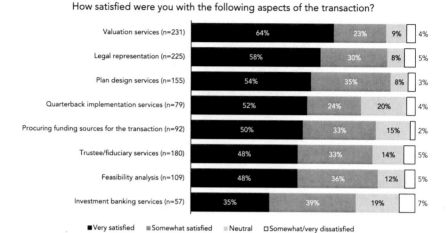

How satisfied were you with the following aspects of the transaction?

	Very satisfied	Somewhat satisfied	Neutral	Somewhat/very dissatisfied
Valuation services (n=231)	64%	23%	9%	4%
Legal representation (n=225)	58%	30%	8%	5%
Plan design services (n=155)	54%	35%	8%	3%
Quarterback implementation services (n=79)	52%	24%	20%	4%
Procuring funding sources for the transaction (n=92)	50%	33%	15%	2%
Trustee/fiduciary services (n=180)	48%	33%	14%	5%
Feasibility analysis (n=109)	48%	36%	12%	5%
Investment banking services (n=57)	35%	39%	19%	7%

■ Very satisfied ■ Somewhat satisfied ■ Neutral □ Somewhat/very dissatisfied

Figure 9-12. Satisfaction with the transaction

Appendix: Survey Questionnaire

Background

Please answer all of the following questions about your initial transaction. If your initial transaction was more than 10 years ago and you have had a subsequent transaction, please base your answers on that most recent transaction.

1. Indicate below if you will be answering the survey about your initial ESOP transaction or a subsequent ESOP stock purchase transaction, and the *YEAR* it took place:

    ⑥ Initial transaction

    ⑥ Most recent transaction

    (Please specify the year it took place) _____

2. What percentage of the company's shares did the ESOP own after that *initial* transaction? Please enter whole numbers only between 0 and 100 without a percentage sign. _____

3. Is your company an S corporation or a C corporation?

    ⑥ S corporation

    ⑥ C corporation

    ⑥ Was a C corporation at the time of the initial transaction, then converted to S corporation

    ⑥ Was a S corporation at the time of the initial transaction, then converted to C corporation

4. What percentage of the company's shares did the ESOP own *before* that transaction? Please enter whole numbers only between 0 and 100 without a percentage sign. _____

5. What percentage of the company's shares did the ESOP own *after* that transaction? Please enter whole numbers only between 0 and 100 without a percentage sign. _____

6. Is your company an S corporation or a C corporation?
   - ⓐ S corporation
   - ⓐ C corporation
   - ⓐ Was a C corporation at the time of this transaction, then converted to S corporation
   - ⓐ Was a S corporation at the time of this transaction, then converted to C corporation

7. Overall, how would you rate the impact of the ESOP on your business?
   - ⓐ Very positive
   - ⓐ Somewhat positive
   - ⓐ Neutral
   - ⓐ Somewhat negative
   - ⓐ Very negative

8. Who was the trustee for the transaction?
   - ⓐ The seller
   - ⓐ Company insider(s) other than seller
   - ⓐ An outside individual
   - ⓐ An outside institution

9. Did you hire someone to serve as a project manager for the whole transaction, i.e., to manage the work of other service providers; to serve as your "quarterback" for the process?
   - ⓐ Yes
   - ⓐ No

10. Which of the following services did the company or trust retain from an outside firm for the transaction? (Check all that apply.)
    - ⓐ Valuation services
    - ⓐ Trustee/fiduciary services
    - ⓐ Investment banking services

ⓖ Feasibility analysis

ⓖ Plan design services

ⓖ Procuring funding sources for the transaction

ⓖ Separate legal representation for the trust

ⓖ Separate legal representation for the company

ⓖ Separate legal representation for the seller(s)

ⓖ Separate advisor to the seller(s)

ⓖ We did not pay an outside firm to do any of these specific services

Please note any other services you paid for not captured in this list. _____

11. **Beyond the transaction valuation, were any of the following additional valuation analyses delivered to the trustee? (Check all that apply.)**

ⓖ Preliminary valuation

ⓖ Fairness opinion

ⓖ Independent review of the valuation

ⓖ Valuation by a second appraisal firm

ⓖ Solvency opinion

ⓖ Quality of earnings report

12. **Approximately how much did the transaction cost in total? (This would include legal, administrative, feasibility, valuation and trustee fees, and any other fees associated with the transaction paid by the company.)**

ⓖ Less than $75,000

ⓖ $75,001 to $125,000

ⓖ $125,001 to $200,000

ⓖ $200,001 to $300,000

ⓖ More than $300,000

13. **Please describe any special circumstances that affected the price of the transaction.** _____

Examples might include unexpected events in the market, changes in the team of service providers, additional analysis, changes in the seller's priorities, complex financing, etc.

14. **Was the ESOP transaction leveraged?**

ⓖ No

ⓖ Yes (please provide the percentage of the transaction that was funded by the loan/s) _____

15. What is/was the length of the senior loan? Please answer in months. _____

16. If the transaction involved a loan, please provide the following information:

	Percentage of the loan (not of the total transaction) financed by each:	Interest rate (nominal—do not take warrants or other factors into account):
The selling owner(s)		
Outside senior debt lender		
Other outside lender/s (mezzanine, subordinate debt, etc.)		

17. Did the transaction involve the seller(s) receiving any warrants, phantom stock, stock appreciation rights, stock options, restricted stock, or any other stock-based or stock-linked securities?

ⓒ Yes

ⓒ No

18. Did the transaction use any of the other following funding methods? (Select all that apply.)

ⓒ Assets were transferred from a pre-existing plan (usually a 401(k) or profit sharing plan)

ⓒ The company pre-funded the plan (by placing cash in the ESOP trust before the transaction)

ⓒ The company provided a cash contribution in the year of the transaction

ⓒ Outside equity investment

ⓒ Management equity investment

ⓒ Other (please specify) _____

19. Did any of the sellers use a 1042 election? (Section 1042 of the Internal Revenue Code allows for deferral of capital gains taxation under certain circumstances.)

ⓒ Yes

ⓒ No

20. Roughly how many months did it take to complete the transaction? (Measure from when the first letter of engagement was signed with a lawyer or other ESOP professional to the completion of the transaction.) _____

21. How satisfied were you with the following aspects of the transaction?

    [For each aspect listed below, respondents could choose "Very satisfied," "Somewhat satisfied," "Neutral," "Somewhat dissatisfied," "Very dissatisfied," or "We did not use this service"]

    Overall

    Legal representation

    Valuation services

    Trustee/fiduciary services

    Feasibility analysis

    Investment banking services

    Plan design services

    Procuring funding sources for the transaction

    Quarterback implementation services

22. Thinking back, what is one thing you wish you had known going into the ESOP transaction? _____

23. What was the total dollar value paid to the seller(s)? (Please provide answer in whole numbers only with no dollar sign)

    From the ESOP _____

    From direct purchasers _____

    From redemptions _____

24. If you don't recall or don't feel comfortable answering the exact amounts, please choose a category below for the *TOTAL* dollar value paid to the seller(s).

    ⑥ Less than $5 million

    ⑥ $5 million up to $25 million

    ⑥ $25 to $35 million

    ⑥ $35 to $50 million

    ⑥ more than $50 million

25. At the time the owner(s) decided to sell shares to the ESOP, was there a potentially credible offer from another party to purchase the company?

    ⑥ Yes, financial buyer

    ⑥ Yes, strategic buyer

    ⑥ Yes, not sure about price

    ⑥ No

26. Please briefly note your main reasons for selling to the ESOP.

    _____

27. Who initially introduced the company to the idea of an ESOP?

    ⑥ The owner

    ⑥ Accountant/CPA

    ⑥ Third party administrator

    ⑥ Financial adviser

    ⑥ Management employee

    ⑥ Non-management employee

    ⑥ Board member

    ⑥ Attorney

    ⑥ ESOP consultant

    ⑥ Investment banker

    ⑥ The National Center for Employee Ownership (NCEO)

    ⑥ Other (please specify) _____

    Finally, please answer a few demographic questions.

28. Which of the below best describes your industry?

    Construction

    Manufacturing

    Wholesale trade

    Retail trade

    Professional, scientific, and technical services

    Financial, insurance, or real estate

    Engineering, architecture, and related fields

    Health care and social assistance

    Technology (computers, biotechnology, software)

    Government contractor

    ⑥ Other (please specify) _____

29. How many employees do you have? (count both full- and part-time employees) _____

30. Where is your company's headquarters?
    State: __ ZIP: _____

31. What was the amount of your company's revenues in the most recently completed fiscal year?
    ⑥ Up to $10 million
    ⑥ $10 million to $50 million
    ⑥ $51 million to $100 million
    ⑥ $101 million to $200 million
    ⑥ $201 million to $500 million
    ⑥ $501 million or more

32. Please provide the company's EBITDA (earnings before interest, tax, depreciation and amortization) as a percentage of revenue in the most recently completed fiscal year:
    ⑥ Negative (we had a loss)
    ⑥ 0–10%
    ⑥ 11–20%
    ⑥ 21% or higher

33. Is your company's stock listed on a public stock exchange?
    ⑥ Yes
    ⑥ No

About the Authors

A graduate of Georgetown University and Boston College Carroll School of Management, **Bill Brett** has spent his entire working career in the field of industrial water treatment. Since 1973, Bill has been employed by Barclay Water Treatment Co., Inc., in Newton, Massachusetts, and for 23 years served as Barclay's president and chief executive officer. In January 2016, Bill stepped down as president and CEO and was elected chair of Barclay's board of directors.

Christopher J. Clarkson is a senior vice president and director in Bernstein's Wealth Planning and Analysis Group. Based in Los Angeles, he has expertise in a variety of complex investment planning issues, including selling a business, diversification of concentrated stock and option portfolios, retirement planning, multigenerational wealth transfer, and philanthropy. Clarkson is a frequent lecturer to groups of tax and legal professionals at continuing education institutes, estate planning councils, charitable organizations, and major accounting and law firms throughout the western United States. He joined Bernstein in 1995 and has been a member of the Wealth Planning and Analysis Group since 1998. Clarkson earned a BA with high honors in business/economics from the University of California, Santa Barbara, and is a Chartered Financial Analyst charterholder.

Ronald J. Gilbert ("Ron") is the cofounder and president of ESOP Services, Inc., an international consulting firm specializing in ESOP transactions. The firm has offices in Virginia and San Diego, with clients throughout the U.S. and internationally. Ron holds a BS from the McIntire School of Commerce at the University of Virginia and a Master of Financial Services from The American College. He currently serves on the ESOP Association's board of governors and its Legislative and Regulatory Advisory Committee, and on the board of directors of four ESOP companies. He is a former NCEO board member. Ron has spoken in nine countries and also has authored many articles on ESOPs. He is a coauthor and coeditor of *Employee Stock Ownership Plans: ESOP Planning, Financing, Implementation, Law and Taxation,* the most comprehensive work on the subject. Ron was instrumental in obtaining the first IRS private letter ruling sanctioning an international ESOP for a U.S.-based company. Before cofounding ESOP Services, Inc., Ron was a vice president of Kelso & Company in San Francisco, working with Louis Kelso, the "father" of the ESOP.

Stacie Jacobsen is a vice president and director in Bernstein's Wealth Planning and Analysis Group. Based in Bernstein's Los Angeles office, she works closely with high-net-worth clients and their professional advisors on a variety of complex planning issues, including multigenerational wealth transfer, philanthropy, liquidity events, and retirement planning. Jacobsen joined the firm in 2001 and began working in the Wealth Planning and Analysis Group in 2004. Jacobsen earned a BS in business administration with an emphasis in finance from the University of Colorado, Boulder, and an MBA from the Marshall School of Business at the University of Southern California.

Nathan Nicholson is a research associate at the National Center for Employee Ownership (NCEO), a private, nonprofit membership, information, and research organization in Oakland, California. The NCEO is widely considered to be the authoritative source on broad-based employee ownership plans. He assists in maintaining and developing the NCEO's research products on employee ownership, including its ongoing surveys of employee-owned companies, analyses of nationwide employee ownership data published by the U.S. Department of Labor, and database of U.S. employee stock ownership plans. He holds a BA from Cornell University.

Loren Rodgers is the NCEO's executive director. Loren joined the NCEO in 2005 after working for 10 years as a consultant to employee-owned companies. He is a frequent speaker and writes extensively on many aspects of employee ownership in professional and academic publications. He works with companies on plan design, operational issues, assessment, governance, communications, and ownership culture. He also consults internationally on employee ownership as public policy. He received his master's degree from the University of Michigan's Institute for Public Policy Studies, where he focused on employee ownership in the United States and in Slavic countries.

Corey Rosen is the NCEO's former executive director and senior staff member. He cofounded the NCEO in 1981 after working for five years as a professional staff member in the U.S. Senate, where he helped draft legislation on employee ownership plans. Before that, he taught political science at Ripon College. He is the author or coauthor of over 100 articles and many books on employee ownership, and a coauthor (with John Case and Martin Staubus) of *Equity: Why Employee Ownership Is Good for Business* (Harvard Business School Press, 2005). He has lectured on employee ownership on six continents, has appeared frequently on CNN, PBS, NPR, MSNBC, and other network programs, and is regularly quoted in the *Wall Street Journal,* the *New York Times, BusinessWeek,* and other leading publications. Corey currently serves on two ESOP company boards and also is on the advisory board of the Certified Equity Professional Institute, the university-based organization that provides the only certification program for equity plan professionals. He previously served on the board of directors of the Great Place to Work Institute (creator of the "The Best 100 Companies to Work for in America" list). In 2009, he was awarded the Txemi Canterra Social Economy Award, given annually in Spain. He holds a PhD in political science from Cornell University.

Paige A. Ryan, using over 25 years of experience in the field of equity compensation and employee ownership, is a driving force behind the consulting services for ESOP Services, Inc., a national consulting firm that assists private and publicly owned companies in designing and implementing successful employee stock ownership plans. She specializes in working directly with business owners to help them analyze and understand the ESOP's impact on the company, shareholders, and employees, focusing on the financial aspects of cash flow, tax savings, shareholder liquidity, and employee benefits. A member of the National Center for Employee Ownership and the ESOP Association, Paige speaks frequently on the topic of ESOPs; teaches a graduate course entitled

"Topics of Corporate Governance: Techniques of Equity Compensation" for the University of California; and writes on the subject. Paige holds a master of international business from the University of San Diego and a bachelor of arts from California State University, Long Beach.

Kenneth E. Serwinski is the cofounder and chairman of Prairie Capital Advisors, Inc., a middle market investment bank and financial advisory firm specializing in ownership transition and the implementation of exit strategies. He has advised companies on over 400 ESOP transactions. Prairie Capital Advisors' expertise in ESOPs includes valuation, structuring, financing, and managing the ESOP process. The firm also provides a varied menu of services for mature ESOP companies.

Brian B. Snarr is a partner at Morrison Cohen LLP in New York and is chair of the firm's Compensation and Benefits Practice Group. His practice includes advising employers, lenders, investors, and fiduciaries on the ERISA, tax, and business law aspects of employee compensation and benefit plans, as well as advising on the ERISA and benefits aspects of the firm's corporate, employment, and transactional practice areas. Mr. Snarr is active in private company ESOP structuring and finance, with substantial experience in the areas of tax and transactional structuring, corporate finance, and ERISA structuring and compliance. He is a member of various professional organizations, has lectured to legal and business audiences on ESOPs and other compensation and benefits topics, and has been quoted on ESOP matters in the business press. He received his BA from Haverford College in 1979 and his JD from the University of Virginia in 1982.

About the NCEO

The National Center for Employee Ownership (NCEO) is widely considered to be the leading authority on employee ownership in the U.S. and the world. Established in 1981 as a nonprofit information and membership organization, it now has more than 3,000 members, including companies, professionals, unions, government officials, academics, and interested individuals. It is funded entirely through the work it does.

The NCEO's mission is to provide the most objective, reliable information possible about employee ownership at the most affordable price possible. As part of the NCEO's commitment to providing objective information, it does not lobby or provide ongoing consulting services. The NCEO publishes a variety of materials on employee ownership and participation; holds dozens of events on employee ownership annually; and offers online courses. The NCEO's work also includes extensive contacts with the media, both through articles written for trade and professional publications and through interviews with reporters.

Membership Benefits

NCEO members receive the following benefits:

- The members-only newsletter *Employee Ownership Report.*
- Access to the members-only area of the NCEO's website, including the NCEO's Document Library for members.
- Free access to live webinars.
- Discounts on books and other NCEO products and services.
- The right to contact the NCEO for answers to questions.

An introductory one-year membership costs $90 for U.S. residents. To join or order publications, telephone us at 510-208-1300 or visit our website at www.nceo.org, which provides news updates and hundreds of articles as well as information on the many ways in which we can assist companies exploring employee ownership.